This book is a treasure! Bankart has written a lovely and loving, practical guide for every man who has struggled with the experience and effects of anger. Compassionate and insightful, he offers constructive suggestions for transforming the energy of anger into a new way of engaging life. I recommend it most highly. Read it—and give it to a man you love.

> —Michael J. Mahoney, professor in the Graduate Department of Holistic Counseling at Salve Regina University and author of *Human Change Processes*

This book is destined to revolutionize anger management theory and practices because of its unique and imaginative blending of Eastern and Western approaches to mastering anger among men. It is a clearly written guidebook filled with practical insights and exercises to control anger problems by integrating Eastern perspectives on consciousness and mindfulness and Western cognitive behavior techniques. Both professionals and those with anger control problems will find this book a welcome change to conventional approaches because of its easy to follow step-by-step methods. This compelling volume could only have been written by an experienced professional and scholar who understands and respects each view. A winner!

> —Anthony J. Marsella, Ph.D., DHC, professor emeritus in the Department of Psychology at the University of Hawaii in Honolulu, HI, and author of numerous books and articles in thee area of cultural and international psychology and psychopathology

D0180489

Since it's virtually the only emotion we're allowed to express, men learn to use anger to express everything—sadness, confusion, despair, frustration. By explaining how men can expand their emotional repertoire, Bankart offers hope for a masculinity that can embrace the full range of emotions—including anger, incidentally. What a valuable resource that is! Finally, we don't just have to get mad. We can get even—even-handed that is.

> —Michael Kimmel, Ph.D., professor of sociology, at the State University of New York, Stony Brook, and author of *Manhood in America*

This work is more than an appropriation of mindfulness or a combination of meditation and cognitive-behavior therapy. It provides an original palette of procedures from various other sources, which, if practiced diligently, have the capacity to strengthen the real weaker sex: angry men. An unmistakable well of inspiration running as a red thread throughout the book forms the Buddha's teachings that emphasize the cultivation of acceptance, kindness, compassion, forgiveness, and humor. Men tormented by self-angering, a largely neglected target group, as well as professionals of both sexes will profit from the rich clinical experience of a seasoned author when healing the typically macho emotion.
On top, readers will gain the invaluable practical insight to foster human interconnectedness that we so much lack in this world. I hope this book will be widely read and thus contribute to have more loving kindness go round on our globe.

> —Maurits G.T Kwee, Ph.D, clinical psychologist, honorary professor at the University of Flores in Buenos Aires, Argentina, and visiting scholar at Waseda University in Tokyo, Japan

Bankart has captured the essence of mindfulness and applied it successfully to one of the most overwhelming and debilitating of human emotions—anger. He is not afraid to acknowledge the contributions of Buddhist psychology to his thinking, but he does so while skillfully weaving the wisdom from Buddhism into a cloth equally fashioned by contemporary Western psychology. Although this book is directed toward the individual who wishes to free himself or herself from the pain and consequences of anger, it also provides a highly accessible yet sophisticated introduction to general principles of Buddhism as a vibrant path to a well-lived life. It is clearly written, easily read— and more importantly, very approachable to both someone struggling with these issues and to therapists working in this area.

—Jean L. Kristeller, Ph.D. professor of psychology at Indiana State University and director of the Center for the Study of Health, Religion, and Spirituality

freeing the angry mind

HOW MEN CAN USE MINDFULNESS & REASON TO SAVE THEIR LIVES & RELATIONSHIPS

C. PETER BANKART, PH.D.

New Harbinger Publications, Inc.

Distributed in Canada by Raincoast Books.

Copyright © 2006 by C. Peter Bankart
New Harbinger Publications, Inc.
5674 Shattuck Avenue
Oakland, CA 94609

Cover design by Amy Shoup; Acquired by Tesilya Hanauer;
Cover image by Stockbyte Platinum/Getty Images;
Text design by Tracy Marie Carlson; Edited by Karen O'Donnell Stein

New Harbinger Publications' Web site address: www.newharbinger.com

Library of Congress Cataloging-in-Publication Data

Bankart, C. Peter, 1946-
   Freeing the angry mind : how men can use mindfulness and reason to save their lives and relationships / C. Peter Bankart.
       p. cm.
   ISBN-13: 978-1-57224-438-2
   ISBN-10: 1-57224-438-0
1. Men—Psychology. 2. Anger. 3. Self-management (Psychology) 4. Interpersonal relations. I. Title.
   HQ1090.B37 2006
   152.4'7081—dc22
                                                                2006007028

08   07   06

10   9   8   7   6   5   4   3   2   1

First printing

Contents

Foreword

Anger appears to be a big part of masculinity in our society. The frequency of this association is disruptive to our society in general (see prison and juvenile-hall population numbers) and to our intimate partner relationships (as evidenced by domestic violence statistics and books about men being from Mars, the god of war). In a lecture I once gave, I said that if there was one thing I would ask about a person in order to predict future aggressiveness, it would be to inquire if they could be described as having psychopathic tendencies. I was made to think twice when an audience member suggested that the most discriminating variable should really be whether or not the person was male. That's not to say that women don't have anger issues, particularly in the realm of relationships—but testosterone and socially indoctrinated images of masculinity still rule when it comes to anger and some of the nastiest expressions of it.

As a result, plenty of people have written books and designed programs to treat men's anger. And there are plenty of excellent exercises and techniques, mostly developed from the carefully researched principles of cognitive behavioral therapy, that have been very helpful in many settings to help men rethink and rework their angry selves.

I have treated men dealing with relationship issues for more than twenty years, and I write books, conduct workshops, and design programs focused on these challenging tasks. And, although I (like most people in this field) believe in giving men very practical and concrete strategies for self-management and personal growth, I haven't had much occasion to try a lot of these techniques myself. But in reviewing this book, I found that several of the interventions really struck my fancy and I decided to give them a whirl. I fell in love with the *sumanai!* exercise. The primary task in this exercise is to generate (and pass on, if appropriate and safe and respectful to the relationship) several profound gratitudes that you feel for an important person in your life. This activity is good, but hardly unique. Unique is the philosophical context in which this simple exercise is placed: *sumanai!*, according to the author, is the Japanese response to a generous act from another person—when most polite Westerners would simply say, "Thank you." *Sumanai!*, instead, means "This is not finished" and it is linked to a complex cycle of obligation and social connection. So I followed the instructions, wrote a brief summary of the concepts, and sent off personalized *sumanai!* gratitude lists to ten of the closest and most loved people in my life. The concluding line in all? "I owe you, and this is not finished." The results were delightful: I was brought to tears several times as I was writing them, reminding myself of the gifts I have received throughout my life from so many. And the responses from my recipients were equally moving (except for those from my teenage kids, who pretended they didn't care, but I know they really did anyway). One male friend of mine urgently wrote back to me making sure that I was okay, and I explained (in the way that guys must joke about serious issues) that I was just having a midlife moment. Not to worry.

And that's what makes this book distinctive: the integration of Buddhist principles and mindfulness strategies into the already well-developed field of anger management. Dr. Bankart insists that men can genuinely develop a different relationship with the universe (and particularly the interpersonal universe closest to them) rather than simply learn some communication techniques and cognitive strategies. He manages to present this complex task through clear, lucid explanations and straightforward, male-user-friendly exercises that can help men truly think about themselves and the world around them differently. Because it is this thinking process, this sense of ourselves as we fit into the interpersonal world, that is the most powerful determinant of prosocial or antisocial behaviors, or even the simplest everyday prorelationship or antirelationship behaviors. Not testosterone. Not evolutionary imperatives. These are important, but (since we have the gift of being *homo sapiens* with well-developed frontal cortexes) not the ultimate determinants of our destiny.

When Dr. Bankart tells us that the only real cure for anger requires a man to "look into his own heart" and "to come to terms with both his own suffering and the ocean of suffering that is in the world all around him," he is letting us know that he is thinking of the big picture, and so must we. Likewise he tells us that he has "written this book to help you save your soul." Refreshingly, the steps along this profound path are not that complicated and can be activated by those of us men who respond best to step-by-step instruction manuals rather than abstract goals.

Perhaps most important of all, in understanding men and relationship breakdowns, is the need to maintain a fundamentally humanistic perspective. Very good men can sometimes behave slightly or even very badly, and this does not necessarily make them bad men (with some obvious exceptions). It makes them (us) flawed men. Join the club. This humanistic perspective reflects the best spirit of the masculine path with heart and the greatest likelihood of actually reaching men. Dr. Bankart tells us that "for every man I've met who celebrates his anger, I've known twenty or thirty or maybe a hundred who were sick at heart that they couldn't figure out how to show the world the thoughtful, loving person they want to be." If this describes you, or describes a man you know and love, then read this book.

—David B. Wexler, Ph.D.
    Executive Director, Relationship Training Institute,
    San Diego, California   www.RTIprojects.com
    Author of *When Good Men Behave Badly: Change Your Behavior, Change Your Relationship* and *Is He Depressed or What: What to Do When the Man You Love Is Moody, Irritable, and Withdrawn*
    July 2005

Introduction

Angry Men Welcome!

Here's a quick checklist to help you see whether this book has the potential to improve your life. How many of the following ten statements do you agree with, in some fundamental way?

- ☐ Anger is making a mess of your life.

- ☐ You want to live long enough to one day be able to hang out with your grandkids.

- ☐ You want to be the sort of person other people look up to and want to be like.

- ☐ Your definition of a hero is a person who can usually keep his cool under pressure.

- ☐ Your greatest rewards in life are living and loving well.

- ☐ You didn't get married with the hope that you'd get divorced too; you didn't have kids so you could see them only on alternate weekends.

☐ Nothing in this world can be or is more important to you than your family.

☐ You hope your kids will grow up wanting to be a lot like you.

☐ Your greatest possessions are your self-respect and your human dignity.

☐ You are unhappy that the people who love you also fear you.

I'm willing to bet that you agreed with almost all of these statements but found yourself thinking that consistently living up to these ideals is a real challenge. Because neither we nor our world is perfect, it can be difficult if not impossible to live our minute-by-minute lives in accordance with what our heads know to be best and our hearts most dearly want. I've counseled altogether too many men who were fairly bewildered by the fact that their kids hated and feared them—but who were also virtually addicted to receiving the "respect" they routinely coerced out of everyone around them. Every one of these guys learned how to be cruel and uncompromising from someone in their own family, and they all talked like they had signed some solemn oath that they would keep their family's anger legacy alive by passing it down to their own children. These are hostile and bitter guys who, though they may spout aphorisms like "Well, maybe the meek will inherit the earth, but they won't get it until I'm done with it!" end up in cardiac intensive care because their lives are painful jumbles.

Of course, if you think that mindless anger makes you a Big Strong Man, if you think your anger is impressive or even a sign of your authority and importance, then you can just put this book down and go find some poor student driver to blow your car horn at. It seems so completely obvious to me that impulsive, senseless anger is destructive and counterproductive that I really can't imagine trying to persuade anyone otherwise. My experience has persuaded me that anger, revenge, fear, hate, and other destructive human emotions are physically and emotionally poisonous.

For every man I've met who celebrates his anger, I've known twenty or thirty or maybe a hundred who were sick at heart that they couldn't figure out how to show the world the thoughtful, loving person they want to be. These are guys who really hate looking in the mirror every morning and seeing a lonely, hostile isolated human being staring back at them. If you have spent too much time being one of these guys, I am glad you are reading this book. I've written it for people who are ready to confront the fact that anger sucks, and who want to learn how to convert their convictions into actions.

WHY I WROTE THIS BOOK

In my thirty-five-year career as a psychologist and a therapist I have logged a lot of hours working with angry men and doing research on anger. In that process I have learned that angry men are hurting. Anger is a powerful and unhealthy emotion, and an angry life is one that is full of physical and emotional pain and frustration. I've also learned that anger is also almost completely unnecessary in everyday life.

The good news is that there are a lot of positive ways to address the anger in your life, and all of them can have real value in helping you become more aware of strategies for bringing your anger under better control. On the other hand, just focusing on how to *manage* your anger leaves too many important questions unanswered. In most cases, simply managing anger doesn't get at the real, deep problem—that anger is a relentless invisible poison that slowly murders a person both physically and spiritually. The simple but profound truth is that the only real *cure* for anger requires a man to look deeply into his own heart and come to terms with both his own suffering and the ocean of suffering that is in the world all around him.

The cure that I am offering is not designed only to help you realize how ridiculous you are when you lose your temper at work or on the road. And I'm not really interested in exploring your past or threatening you with dire consequences if you don't mend your ways. Instead, this therapy involves a kind of psychological open-heart surgery; it is based on a very deep conviction that angry men need to reawaken their sense of what it means to be a mortal human being—a being who lives in a world where everyone's very survival depends on his or her connections with other human beings. This cure asks you, in the most basic way you can imagine, to clear your mind, respect your physical being, and open your heart. The real key to this approach is for you to actively decide to *refuse to be a creature of your own anger*.

Just Say No to Anger!

Being an angry person is a lot like being a nicotine addict. Do you know how just about everyone who quits using tobacco does it? They *just quit* (Prochaska 1999). With no patches, no hypnosis, no psychotherapy, no surrendering to a Higher Power. They just look those disgusting cancer sticks in the eye—and they tell them to go to hell. They *just quit*. With anger, as with smoking, the only way to get over your problem is to look it square in the eye and *just quit*.

In order to successfully change anything important about your existence you essentially have to look at yourself in the mirror and firmly declare that you are going to take charge of your life. You have to declare that you are tired of being jerked around by something that is bad for you and harms the people around you. Like a two-pack-a-day smoker giving up tobacco, you will find the path difficult and extremely challenging at times, and you will probably have a few relapses. You will probably run into situations where you discover that your bad behavior has become automatic, and you will find yourself still acting like a tool of your bad habits.

But this isn't brain surgery! Chances are that nobody is going to die if you screw up as you go through this trial-and-error process of changing into a better human being. When you mess up, and particularly when you mess up pretty badly, you'll need to pick yourself up, brush the dust off your pride, and get back on the horse. You have to believe in yourself and remember that if you pay attention to what you are doing, there is nothing that can stop you from achieving what you have set out to do—even though when you are up to your ass in alligators, as they say, it can be pretty difficult to remember that your objective is to drain the swamp. Of course, alligators or no, if you aren't serious about change, you're only fooling yourself. You may not be fooling others, however: although most people will admire you for talking about trying to reform, 99 percent of them won't actually believe that you are serious about it (or that you have what it takes to accomplish anything that serious) until they see some proof.

Finding a Pathway Out of Anger

Here is something that might surprise you. Reading this book will not make you less of a pain in the neck to love, live with, work with, or sit next to at your kid's Little League game. It would be nice if it were that easy, but if that were the case this book would have magic properties and I'd be sitting on my own private beach somewhere contemplating a tropical sunset. All a book can offer is a set of ideas, a whole bunch of suggestions, and a pathway to a different kind of life. If this book is really successful it might even make you feel inspired from time to time, but it can't make you get off your butt and become a better human being.

This book has been written, therefore, for any man who understands what it means to hear and recognize the yearnings of his heart, and who is sincerely looking for a clear way to transform the angry thoughts and dark emotions that have hardened his heart, corrupted his body, and clouded his mind. I hope to show you a practical, natural, and trustworthy path that will help you transform your angry impulses into experiences that help you become more fully human once again. It doesn't matter whether you are the most religious person in the world or the most outspoken atheist in your neighborhood; I've written this book to help you save your soul.

As a fundamental starting point, take some time out of the grind of your daily routine to remind yourself that, like all human beings, you are mortal. Moreover, because you are a mere mortal, you have been given a very limited amount of time on this earth. It is crucial, therefore, that you start *right now* paying a lot more attention to the quality of your life. It is especially urgent that you begin to actively open your eyes to the quality of your most important human relationships. One of the fundamental teachings in Buddhist philosophy is that human beings really only exist because they share their lives with other human beings. This is the same idea that was voiced by the English poet John Donne, who observed that no man is an island, and no man is complete unto himself (1962). The bottom line is that if you seek release from the prison of your own emotional instability, you must accept that your very life depends on your connections with others.

A LITTLE BIT OF THEORY

The guiding principles in the approach to managing stress and controlling anger given in this book come from three different-looking but actually very similar sources.

Buddhism Applied to Everyday Life

The first of these sources is the philosophical wisdom of the Buddha, who, though he was a religious hermit who lived in a remote northern Indian forest twenty-five hundred years ago, had some important and relevant things to say about anger. The Buddha really didn't talk at all about what we would consider to be religion; his teachings were primarily concerned with how ordinary people could live a life that is both purposeful and free from suffering. The most powerful insight contained in all of the Buddha's teaching is that all human beings inevitably inhabit a life that is halfway between heaven and hell: it is full of suffering but it is also full of bliss. The *only* effective response to all that suffering is *compassionate concern for all living things;* the experience of bliss is the experience of compassion.

Developing Mindful Self-Awareness

The second source is the life-enhancing practice of mindfulness, a way of being in and interacting with the world that significantly reduces stress and promotes physical and emotional well-being. The idea of mindfulness is actually quite simple: it means paying attention purposefully, in a particular way. That particular way involves remaining in the present moment and steadfastly holding one's mind open, without judgment.

Once you have learned how to pay mindful attention, you will have a significantly greater appreciation of what is actually going on in the world all around you. With that fresh awareness you will become free to enter into that world with deliberate intent (Brown and Ryan 2003).

At the heart of this book, then, is a series of mindfulness exercises, all of which are designed to make you more aware of your physical self, your mental processes, and your relationships with other people. These exercises are called "meditations" because they are designed to help you focus your awareness in a deliberate and meaningful way on some aspect of reality that you may have stopped paying close attention to. With practice you can become more mindful of just about everything in your life. You can, for example, slow down while eating and become aware of the appearance, texture, temperature, and taste of everything you put in your mouth. The point is not to take an hour and a half to eat your lunch, but to enable yourself to *decide* to pay attention to what you are eating, how it tastes, and whether you really want to eat more of it.

Mindfulness and the meditation exercises that support this practice will give you a greater sense of control over your emotional, verbal, and thought processes. Once you have begun to practice mindfulness on a regular basis in a number of different areas of your life, you will discover that your waking life is made up of dozens and maybe even hundreds of choices every day. Becoming more self-aware, more intentional, and more focused in your daily life will allow you to see the choices you make—such as eating, making love, playing with your kids, greeting your coworkers, or exercising—and, over time, anger will probably be a choice you make far less often.

Try this simple exercise in mindfulness to see if it makes sense to you. Select a very small piece of food that you enjoy but don't think about a whole lot. Mindfulness expert Jon Kabat-Zinn asks people to eat a raisin. In my work I like to ask people to try a berry; other folks like to sample a nice piece of chocolate. If you are brave, try a chunk of jalapeño pepper. Just make it something fairly routine, something you no longer pay much attention to.

Begin by examining this thing very carefully with your eyes, and then your nose. Explore it quite carefully. Now place it on the tip of your tongue, and just let it sit there. Experience the taste sensation, but also experience its shape, texture, and temperature. Feel what the heat from your mouth does to this little morsel; press it against the roof of your mouth with your tongue. Let its flavor fill your entire mouth; notice how your salivary glands have brightened up at the news that food is present. When you are ready, chew and swallow, and trace the sensation of swallowing right down your throat. Hold the sensation and the feeling for a minute or two.

Now, focus on what memories, feelings, and emotions are present in your mind, all triggered by this simple little mindful meditation. With the berry, people often remember the experience of picking berries on hot summer days when they were kids, and the smell of homemade pies cooking. Or perhaps they remember the sharpness of the thorns on the raspberry canes, and the mosquito bites they endured while picking enough berries for a pie. There is a world of sensory and emotional experience wrapped inside that berry, and becoming aware of that experience is what mindful meditation is all about. It means being fully aware, on purpose, in the present moment, of one's own natural experience.

Cognitive Behavioral Therapy

The third important source of principles in this book is cognitive behavioral therapy. CBT, as we psychologists refer to it, is the most effective form of psychotherapy to come down the pike since they stopped drilling holes in people's heads to release the demons that they thought caused madness. If you want to know what psychotherapists dream about, it is that one day, perhaps in the not-too-distant future, CBT will completely replace medications as everyone's first-choice treatment method for emotional and behavioral problems.

CBT operates on a very simple premise: that how we act, and how we feel, depend almost exclusively on how we think. Thousands of good research studies support the effectiveness of CBT, and it is the only therapy that not only works virtually all the time with just about every sort of client and emotional problem but also continues to work once therapy is over—all without any unhappy side effects. The only problem with CBT is that it tends to tell you that you have to think rationally, but it doesn't really tell you what rational thinking is.

Combining All Three Approaches

The philosophy of Buddhism, the practice of mindfulness, and the rational guidance of CBT converge to contribute one fundamental idea behind this project. The Buddha taught that a good and well-lived life is one sincerely devoted to the reduction of suffering—in ourselves as well as in others. Mindfulness shows us that in order to regain control over our lives we must learn how to pay careful and close attention to what we are thinking, feeling, saying, and doing. CBT allows us to see that our anger is rooted in the nutty and warped ways we have been thinking about our daily experiences. Of course, after you come to see yourself and your world more clearly, immediately, and rationally, you can still *choose* to be a jerk; nobody can really stop you. But chances are that, because you are an aware human being, you will choose to use your newfound ability to think and see clearly and behave compassionately; you will *choose* to do everything in your power to reduce the suffering that exists in yourself and in this world.

Let me be plain—I don't believe all this just because it is a nice theory. I believe it because I am a very practical psychologist who has spent his life working with a bunch of hard-headed, practical men whom I have seen change as a result of putting into practice the ideas that you will encounter in this book (Bankart 1997, 2002). I believe in this approach for one very basic reason: *it works!*

But there is one catch. This program only works if you actually *do* it. It is not just a matter of believing in its concepts and thinking they're a really good idea. You can't accomplish the goals of this program by sitting around and saying, "I really *must* put compassion, mindfulness, and rational thinking on my to-do list someday." Effecting these changes requires significant work on your part. Success is, ultimately, a matter of daily *practice*.

THE BIG IDEA: PRACTICE AND AWARENESS

The big idea at the heart of this book is this: to change your life in a significant way, it is not enough for you just to think about and want to change; you must also practice, practice, practice.

The teachings of the Buddha, the principles of mindfulness, and the data that support CBT are in complete agreement that the *only* way you can significantly improve the quality of your life is to deliberately live your day-to-day and even moment-to-moment existence in a very specific way. This book is your brief introduction to that "way." When you follow this program you will discover it to be completely natural and actually not all that difficult. But you have to live and experience these practices directly, immediately, and with open-eyed attention and awareness every single day of your life.

The problem most of us face, of course, is that we live our lives almost completely absentmindedly. We run around on automatic pilot, letting old habits take over our brains and our hearts. Far too much of the time we live our daily lives in a kind of mindless fog; our thinking is cluttered, and our attention is divided. We respond to the world in tired old ways—we are unconscious of the choices we are making and of the alternatives we haven't chosen. We are almost never fully aware of the potential in our every waking moment. Buddhists like to say that trying to make sense of the world with an undisciplined mind is the equivalent of having a drunken monkey running around inside our heads. The goal of this anger reduction project (this book) is to sober that monkey up and teach him some manners.

HOW TO USE THIS BOOK

The anger management program set out in this book comprises three parts: the text, the exercises, and the Anger Control Journal.

The Book

You can either read the book from start to finish and then go back and work on the exercises and the journal activities chapter by chapter, or you can work through the book chapter by chapter. It is probably best to take the chapters in order (not skipping around), because the material in each successive chapter will make more sense after you have mastered the material in the previous chapter.

Nobody likes to be told what to do, and I hope you won't find yourself feeling lectured as you read this book. Rather, what you will find here are dozens of suggestions and ideas for how to improve your life and enrich the quality of your relationships with other people. To invite you to think a bit about the main points in this book I've included a large number of parables and anecdotes. Many of them are humorous, some are autobiographical, and a lot are traditional "teaching stories" passed down from Buddhist teachers over the last thousand years. Most people find that the ideas they learn from stories are the lessons they remember long after they have finished reading a book, so I hope you will find the stories herein both interesting and thought provoking. When you find one that you really like, try telling it to a few other people, to make them think and laugh too. It turns out that the biggest impact from a good teaching story often comes from the retelling.

The Exercises

The heart and soul of this program is a series of exercises designed to open your eyes to the realities inside your head and all around you. This new awareness will transform the way you treat yourself and interact with the rest of the world. It will, basically, give you an opportunity to resume the long-delayed project of growing up to become a mature, responsible, and loving adult.

The exercises suggested in each chapter are designed to build on each other. Some of them will be more difficult than others, but regardless of how difficult or easy you find them they all need to be completed and in many cases practiced on a regular basis. An important part of the overall program depends on your becoming more self-disciplined, more self-aware, and much more in control of your thought processes and emotions. Simply wishing you were better at these things doesn't work. What does work is effort, organization, and determination. You can't skip the exercises or do them halfheartedly and still expect to benefit from the program.

Your Anger Control Journal

Many of the exercises involve creating and maintaining an Anger Control Journal, a structured personal log in which you will record careful observations about a great many details of your life that relate to your anger and your emotional well-being. From time to time you will be asked to share the contents of your journal with your spouse or partner or kids, and you will also be asking them to give you information that you can include in your journal. The journal is a permanent record of your progress toward controlling your anger and improving the quality of your life.

To begin your journal you will need to either create a new computer file or purchase a notebook that you will use exclusively for this project.

THE PRINCIPLE OF *RIGHT EFFORT*

In the ancient Buddhist catechism of moral precepts (called The Noble Eight-Fold Path), the principle of Right Effort is essential whenever you are working on anything important. Moreover, since in Buddhism everything a person does is important, Right Effort is really required in every aspect of your daily life. Therefore, you need to be *attentive, serious, dutiful,* and *patient* as you work on the various exercises in this book. Because this is your life, and because you are committed to making important and lasting changes in that life, you need to become as *obsessively thorough* as you can be with each step of the program.

When you find yourself backsliding (and you almost certainly will), you will need to go back far enough in the program to a place where you can once again stand on solid ground. Once you have regained your confidence and reconnected with your inner supply of determination, you will be ready to begin moving forward once again. (This is, of course, another reason why you should complete the chapters and exercises in order.)

Regardless of why anger has become a destructive force in your life, you are about to make a serious commitment to go through a significant change process. The lesson is clear: if you can make up your mind to change, you will be successful. All you really have to do is pay close attention to yourself, follow the instructions in this book, and have a little faith in your ability to succeed. With any luck at all you will have lots of good people on your side, encouraging you to kick the anger habit—and only a few guys cheering you on to exercise your God-given right to be as big a jerk as you can possibly be. But first, you need to take stock of your life.

Now, take a deep breath, turn the page, and let's begin.

1

Taking Charge, Taking Responsibility

My phone was already ringing when I got to my office early one morning last fall. "Hey, it's me!" cracked a familiar voice on the other end of the line. "I really need some help."

It was my friend Steve, a former client, and now the proud daddy of two little boys. Only this time Steve wasn't calling me to share his son's latest misadventure at school or news of the baby's newest word.

Steve's voice was choked with tears. He was in big trouble. He needed help—and it couldn't wait. Steve told me he was standing in his kitchen, and I could almost feel him shaking with fear and rage. He had stripped the leather belt off his pants and it was now clenched in one fist while he gripped the phone in the other. Steve said he was almost physically sick with fear. He was just about to beat his son for the first time.

There had been a disagreement over breakfast. It had started with a dispute over whether five-year-old Christopher would wear the clothes that his mom had laid out before she left for work. Christopher was adamant: he was *not* going to wear that shirt to kindergarten. Steve was equally adamant: Christopher would *do as he was told*. Within five minutes something akin to hell on earth had broken loose.

Had *Steve* ever refused to wear the shirt that *he* had been told to wear, his dad would have ended the argument with a swift and serious beating. That, and a million other little and not-so-little things, were what had brought Steve to my psychotherapy practice six years earlier, an angry and bewildered young man who was beginning to realize that he had no idea how to live his own life.

Now it was Steve's turn to hold the belt; it was Steve's responsibility to make the decisions that would shape a young life. He was more globally disturbed at that moment in his life than he had ever been before in his twenty-five years.

Everything in Steve's background told him that Christopher's defiance could only be met with anger and violence. It was time for Christopher to learn that when a man gives an order, and when that man has power, he has the right to use righteous pain to make certain that his will is strictly enforced. It was Christopher's time to learn that anger, fear, and physical pain are the ultimate tools that real men use to get their way. Welcome to the world of men, Christopher.

But in the split second it took for Steve to remove his belt, a whole lot of things that Steve and I had spent so long working out together suddenly came into sharp focus. At the height of his fury Steve somehow found the presence of mind to pause for a moment and punch my number on his speed dial, making a phone call that would change his future.

All I did was ask him one question: "Steve, are you convinced that wearing some damned shirt to kindergarten is worth even a half second of the pain you are causing by breaking faith with that little human being in your kitchen?"

Of course it wasn't. It wasn't even close.

Hanging up the phone and giving himself thirty seconds to cool off, Steve squired Christopher to the time-out corner, found an Indiana Basketball shirt in his closet, and two minutes later was hugging his son as if both of their lives depended upon it.

Because, of course, they did.

THE DILEMMA OF *DUKKHA*: "ALL LIFE IS SUFFERING"

Judging from the amount of ordinary human unhappiness (what Buddhists call *dukkha*) that swirls around in our day-to-day lives, I'm convinced that there must be a whole lot of people who, far too often, have mornings like Steve and Christopher's. At the very moment you are reading this, millions of folks, all pretty much just like you, are living in a state of chronic unhappy, angry distress. A huge proportion of these unhappy souls are men who spend much of their waking hours experiencing and expressing chronic anger. Most of these people seem to have no self-awareness of how much pain and unhappiness they are in, let alone how much suffering they are mindlessly causing others.

It is easy to get the impression that angry people think making other human beings frustrated, upset, and afraid is an ordinary and normal thing. Some of them even create the impression that they enjoy being miserable, and more than a few seem to have developed a perverse knack for passing their anger along to the people around them. Because they are so wrapped up in the misery of their daily lives, many of them may become addicted to the adrenaline surge they get from inflicting power trips on others.

As Buddhism makes us aware, our lives are constantly flooded with dukkha. We are incredibly vulnerable to sorrow and loss; we fear our fears and despise our enemies. We are lonely and yet we push people away from us. We are leaves being blown about by the winds of our depression, our resentments, our memories of past wrongs and injustices. For many men, anger is the clearest manifestation of dukkha, but rather than confront it some men seem to revel in it.

Too often, the result of all this unexamined suffering is a cynical acceptance of the advice offered by old Prince Machiavelli (2003): that it is better to be feared than to be loved, and that coerced respect is the mark of a natural leader. Perhaps angry men haven't thought about the ramifications of their behavior, or perhaps they just don't care, but chances are there will be more than a few sighs of relief when word gets out that they have suddenly keeled over—probably in the middle of some tirade about how *nobody is any damned good.*

As I pointed out in the introduction, helping you figure out what to do with all this dukkha, all that anger inside you, is why I've written this book.

Taking Stock as if Your Life Depended on It (Because It Does!)

In order to really start getting a handle on your anger and all the dukkha in your life, you must be willing to take stock of your existence. Honest stock taking can be difficult and even painful, but it is better to do it now than to put it off until things become truly disastrous. You have to get beyond the fact that a few people seem to go out of their way to make your life difficult. The real issue is that you make your own life difficult. However, the good news is that, since most of your troubles are of your own making, they are almost completely under your personal control.

You can't escape the fact that you are messing up your own life and the lives of a bunch of other folks because you don't know how to think clearly and control yourself when you are frustrated and stressed. Moreover, you may be headed for an early grave, and with the way things are going there may be an embarrassingly small number of people at your funeral. There are undoubtedly a number of reasons why anger has become an issue in your life. Chances are that you come from a long line of angry, unhappy people. In fact it would be very surprising if anger did not frequently take a prominent place at your family's dinner table when you were a kid. It's also likely that people (and especially the men) in your family got what they wanted when they exercised their tempers. Maybe the only time you could tell what your dad was thinking or feeling was when he was angry. It's likely that some neuroscientist could confirm that you inherited an "angry gene" or two—that it is your nature to be a "hot responder."

But the stock taking that you need to do at this point in your life is not an archeological dig into your family's history. The inventory you need to conduct is located in the here and the now, in your current relationships, and especially in your family. This stock taking is about taking responsibility, not assigning blame. It's a matter of figuring out how you stack up with respect to five basic areas of your life where anger is likely to be rooted.

FIVE BASIC RULES FOR STARTING TO BE A LESS ANGRY PERSON

There are just five common-sense, basic rules you need to follow if you want to gain a major amount of control over your anger. And, frankly, if you can't manage these ground rules, I think you may have to conclude that you simply aren't ready to give up the rights and privileges that go along with the title of certified angry potentate. If this is the case maybe you can donate this book to somebody with a little more determination.

Rule 1: Alcohol Is Not Your Friend

If you don't drink or use mind-altering chemicals of any sort, you can skip this step. But for most angry men the first step in achieving control over anger is getting a solid grip on their use of alcohol and other substances. Because our brains are wired to produce a massive amount of the neurotransmitter dopamine when we consume intoxicants, and because it's so easy to get hooked on that dopamine high, getting firm control of your alcohol and drug use might very well be the toughest challenge in this entire book.

You need to face, as directly as possible, what happens when you drink too much, and what messages your brain sends when it wants a fix. Dopamine is normally responsible for how we feel when we are happy and sexy and full of enthusiasm for life. But if you're an alcoholic, the lack of dopamine is what makes you get out of bed in the morning—to search for your first drink, and dopamine fix, of the day. When you don't get that fix, your nervous system has a tantrum, and you will experience that tantrum as a powerful craving. So, you need to sort out just who is in charge when it comes to your body's dopamine cravings—your will or your biology. In later chapters I give you some ways to coax your dopamine back into the service of your well-being. Regardless, at this point you need to honestly and courageously confront your relationship with alcohol and other substances as it stands at this moment in your life.

I am not telling you that you have to completely quit drinking in order to begin the journey of transformation from Pretty Much a Jerk to Compassionate Human Being. But then again, after honestly considering the details of your own situation, you might decide that quitting is a necessary and important initial step, especially if you tend to engage in binge drinking. The bottom line of rule 1 is that getting over your anger problem is going to require a clear head. You can't go through this process with your mind clouded by alcohol or any other intoxicating substance.

Journal Exercise 1-1: Alcohol and Your Anger

(If you are involved with a problematic substance other than alcohol, modify this exercise accordingly.)

1. In your anger journal or computer file, write down a list of the last ten times (or the most significant ten times) that your temper caused you some significant problems. If all of the items on your list occurred just yesterday, then make your list a bit longer. You want your list to represent, with painful clarity, a significant portion of your recent anger history. For example, you might write, "Some idiot cut me off on the freeway on my way to work this morning."

2. Circle (or set in boldface) each of those angry episodes that had any relation whatsoever to alcohol. If you're courageous, dare to ask your spouse, partner, and/or best friend whether they think alcohol played any part in your handling of these situations. Listen carefully, and then write down their answers. After examining your list and identifying alcohol-related events, you might write something like "Okay, I was a little hungover, and I hadn't gotten much sleep."

3. Now write down what you make of all this. You might ask yourself what kind of person people would perceive you as if they could see the real you, not just the angry person they fear. You might also ask yourself what the truth is about the relationship between your alcohol use and your interactions with other people. Your answer might be something like the following: "I guess it's true that I'm hungover in the morning a lot. Plus, lack of sleep leaves me really irritable."

4. Write a letter to Mr. Alcohol that sets him straight about who is in charge in your relationship. This is an exercise that many anger management clients have found very useful. In your letter, be truthful and passionate, and take this opportunity to do the following:

    ■   Acknowledge your past relationship with alcohol.

    ■   Assess your current relationship.

    ■   Clearly and forcefully define your future relationship.

The most important aspect of this letter is the part where you declare your refusal to let a bunch of organic molecules define and destroy your peace of mind and your relationships with other human beings. It's all about being a hero. The last sentence of your letter might read something like this: "Al, it's been a hell of a ride. But hey, big guy, it's over."

Rule 2: "Masculinity" Is Not a Valid Justification for Anger!

Back in the 1970s psychologists half-joked that all male brains were testosterone poisoned. Not to be outdone, others countered that female brains were even more seriously disabled by PMS. According to this pseudoscientific logic, men could be as aggressive and angry as they wanted to be and women could act as unpleasant and irritable as they wished, and nobody would be responsible because it was all just hormones. But you know that no judge or jury will even think about patting you on the head and sending you on your way if you try to pass off illegal and dangerous behavior as a result of hormone poisoning. Neither common sense nor the science of brain chemistry will back you up.

It's not that testosterone is irrelevant in how you perceive the world. However, it is never a valid excuse for not exercising self-control and for permitting yourself to act like a jerk. There may be a slight correlation between testosterone surges and competitive, aggressive behavior in men (although these links are probably not as clear or as strong as some people would like to think), but all that really means is that, like a very tall visitor to a kindergarten class, you have to pay really close attention to where you are walking.

Unfortunately, some degree of anger justification is built in to the definition of masculinity in many North American and Western European subcultures. Anger justification probably plays a pretty huge role in the definition of masculinity in prisons and among male adolescents and some professional athletes. So if you are an adolescent professional athlete in jail for beating your girlfriend senseless with your hockey stick, you probably really are to some degree a victim of your culture's peculiar definition of what it means to be a "normal" human male.

But what about the rest of us? What about all of us grown-up guys who have jobs and families and aren't paid to hammer the crap out of other people? Probably the toughest challenge in being a Big Strong Man is accepting the fact that somewhere along the way someone (probably your dad, if you need to assign blame) taught you a whole lot of horrible junk about what it means to be a "real" man—and acknowledging that all that junk is now threatening just about everything you honor and treasure in your life. If you sincerely believe that a real man is a person who dominates weaker men, small children, and women, then I respectfully ask you to look at yourself in the mirror and ask yourself who the heck you are trying to impress. Do you really believe that a "real man" has to control other people through fear and intimidation? Is anger really the best emotion to use to protect your family from all the dangers and horrors that exist in the world? Have you ever witnessed an actual guy losing his temper and said to yourself, "Now there's a real man"? When you explode at some poor slob who is an incompetent driver or can't figure out how to give correct change at the grocery store checkout line, are people gathering around and asking their sons to admire you, a great example of a real man?

Journal Exercise 1-2:
The Lessons You Learned About Anger

1. Your next journal assignment is to write out a complete inventory of everything you have ever learned about anger. Your self-justification system will probably look something like this:

    "If you know you are right, you are entitled to demand that people shut up, listen to you, and do what you say."

"If I've had to take a lot of crap at work today, people had better not get on my bad side when I get home."

2. Include, as best you can, an analysis of when, where, and from whom you learned those lessons.

3. Pay very special and close attention to what you have been taught about the connection between anger and masculinity. Does being a man give a person special permission to lose his temper? Is anger a manly way to interact with other people?

4. Make a phone call to a sibling to ask about what lessons about justifying anger he or she remembers learning during childhood. Analyze how similar or dissimilar your sibling's anger lessons are to your own.

5. Ask your kids what lessons you've taught them about anger. Ask them what they think about your excuses for getting angry.

Take your time with this exercise, and give it some careful thought. You probably won't be able to remember everything the first time you sit down to do it, so leave lots of extra room for adding information later if you are using a notebook. Please do not judge or evaluate this list! If your grandpa said that no man should tolerate disrespect from his kids, then just note that down. Don't editorialize. But do make sure that you identify as many details as you can remember about Grandpa's lesson.

The point here is not that all of these rules are worthless—it is this: You were raised with a certain set of beliefs, attitudes, and values about anger. And since these beliefs are constantly rattling around inside your head, you might as well put them down on paper so you can study them mindfully.

Rule 3: No Excuses

One of the things that gets in the way of angry people's progress is that they tend to have lots of excuses that justify their being the way they are. Of course, some angry people don't have any sincere desire to stop being angry. These are the guys who were spoiled rotten by their parents and who now think that their possession of a penis permits them to be the tyrant boss of everyone else on the planet. But even the people who realize how destructive their anger is, and who really want to change, can come up with one hundred trillion excuses for losing their temper and exploding at some poor soul who just happened to be in the wrong place at the wrong time.

Here's the simple truth: There is no excuse for not being the person you want to be. There is no excuse for doing things that you don't want to do. There are no excuses for making your child cry, your spouse despise you, or your coworkers fear you. No excuses. *None.* I don't care if you *have* told him eight thousand times not to leave his bike in the driveway. His mistake may be reason enough for you to take away his bike for the next week or month, but it is not an excuse for you to act like a martyred prophet whose word has been violated in direct contradiction to the very command of God Herself.

No Excuses is a very powerful, yet very difficult, rule to live by. Angry people, much like everyone else, live in a fantasy world of self-justification. They seem to want everyone to believe something like "I don't lose my temper; other people steal it from me!" They seem to think that if every single person in the known universe would do exactly what they want them to, then they would allow the world to exist in peace. Once the entire universe was lined up precisely the way they wanted it to be, then, they promise, they would never, never, never have to lose their temper and act like a complete idiot again. But of course that rule only works as long as they are the only people who get to have their each and every dumb wish granted. And chances are that that is not going to happen, at least in this lifetime.

The key to understanding the excuse system of angry people is the recognition that angry people, with all their rules and commandments, tend to have a gigantic problem with one of the most common words in the English language: *but.*

- "I came home from work in a good mood today, thinking about playing some ball with you, *but* there was your bike in the driveway . . ."

- "I was going to ask you if you wanted to make love after the kids were in bed tonight, *but* then you told me that you had forgotten the dry cleaning . . ."

- "All I want is a little peace and quiet, *but* you just can't leave me alone for ten minutes . . ."

- "You know the rule about finishing your homework before you watch television, *but* you chose to defy me . . ."

So, what's going on here? The answer is that angry people set up the world with a million logical trip wires—microscopic rules that other people *must* live by if they are to have any hope whatsoever of staying on your nice side. You would play catch with your son, *if* he had remembered about his bike. You'd make love to your partner, *if* she had remembered to do those errands. You'd have been a ball of fun after dinner, *if* the world had given you fifteen minutes to unwind when you got home from work. You'd let your kids watch their favorite show *if* they obeyed your holy commandment about homework. People keep stealing your humanity from you!

Look, I'm all for the kid being responsible for his bike, and I sympathize with your frustration over the clean shirt you needed for that meeting tomorrow, and I get that you had a long, hard day at work. However, I do want to point out that lashing out at the poor unfortunate souls who have to live with you is not doing one damned thing to get them to obey your rules. It's not working. Get it? You can make them fear you, but you can't make them remember and obey all the rules all the time. Moreover, if you think back to your own childhood, or to the last time (heaven forbid!) that *you* screwed up, you will remember how it felt when somebody got mad at you: it completely shut down whatever sincere regret you felt over screwing up.

Here's the key point: you can't let other people's screwups become your excuse for screwing up too! What's worse: the fact that your true love forgot the dry cleaning, or that you forgot your promise that you were really, really going to try to stop being an asshole? That's a serious question.

Here's a simple (but perhaps a little difficult) tip to help you stop using excuses. For the next week of your life, eliminate the word *but* from your vocabulary. Every single time you want to use that word, substitute the word *and*. This exercise, adapted from the work of Steve Hayes and his colleagues at the University of Nevada at Reno, is essentially a mindfulness meditation on the way we use language to create and bolster our excuse systems (Hayes, Strosahl, and Wilson 1999). Here's how those statements might sound with *and* instead of *but*:

■ "I have asked him a million times not to leave his bike in front of the garage doors, *and* all that bitching at him hasn't done any good at all. We need to find some rational way to solve this problem."

■ "I'd really like to make love with my partner tonight, *and* I have to figure out what I am going to wear to that meeting tomorrow. And, you know, thinking about sex is a lot more enjoyable than thinking about work."

■ "I'm really burned out from work right now, *and* if you can give me ten minutes of peace and quiet then maybe we can take the dog for a walk before dinner."

■ "I thought we had an agreement about television and homework, *and* I expect you to finish your homework before you start watching your show."

Journal Exercise 1-3: *But* Out—*and* In

1. In your journal, write down your own three favorite *but*isms right now.

2. Try substituting *and* in these three *but* statements.

3. Observe the emotional difference this change makes possible. Write down the feelings and thoughts associated with the *but* statements; then write down how those feelings change when you turn those thoughts into *and* statements.

4. Now, go back to the list of recent anger-related incidents that you compiled in journal exercise 1-1. Take one or two of these incidents that seem freshest in your mind, and see if you can recall how you used the word *but* in those situations. Substitute *and* for *but* and note how the situation might have changed given that substitution.

The next time you begin to get angry, immediately plug the word *and* into your thinking box and see what a difference it makes. Record your experience in your journal.

Rule 4: You Are Not Your Anger!

This rule might sound a little easier to follow than the first three, but it will probably be more of a challenge than you imagine. Rule 4 requires you to develop a special kind of double consciousness. You need to learn how to become an active and objective observer of your self. This will allow you to begin seeing yourself as other people see you. As we learned earlier in this chapter, it can be really difficult to recognize that the person we project to others is sometimes very different from the person we believe ourselves to be. Hardly anyone wants to project an image of an angry tyrant, because hardly anyone thinks of himself that way. But accurate self-perception is almost completely lost when we are overtaken by anger, so we end up behaving in ways that are different from our self-image, as a loving and reasonable human being.

When you are literally at your worst, when your anger is almost out of control, is that creature really *you?* Of course, it is you in a physical sense—it is your body, your voice, your passionate response to the situation (and your excuse system, too!). But is that the person you really are? Is that the same guy who loves his wife deeply, who would sacrifice his life for his kids without thinking about it twice, and who truly cares about the well-being of others?

Seen from a mindful perspective, anger is an active choice. It is a road that a person *does not have to take.* Of course, one of the problems with that choice is that, like getting on the wrong freeway, by the time you realize your error it's difficult to change your direction. That being said, you can *choose to become mindful* even in the midst of your own temporary breaks with sanity. Even in the midst of a perfect storm of awful thoughts and angry impulses you do have the ability to shift the focus of your attention away from your emotions, and even away from the target of your anger. In later chapters of this book you will learn some ways you can practice this in your daily life, but for now just appreciate that you can get to a place where anger becomes a *choice* that you make, not a path you are compelled to take.

The path of anger is *always* the path of suffering, of dukkha. Anger increases suffering in at least four important ways. First, like alcohol and drugs, it destroys your peace of mind by seriously interfering with your ability to think clearly and act effectively. Second, it wrecks your health and confirms to your enemies that you really are a mindless idiot. Third, it has a powerful negative effect on the person you are angry at. It might make them cry, it might make them belligerent, or it might make them try to escape. But what it *won't* do is encourage them to listen to what you are saying and try to figure out how to make a bad situation a little bit better. Fourth, it adds a few drops of poison to the cup that we all have to drink from. Your anger makes being a fellow human being a little less wonderful. It degrades any hope of connection I might want to experience with you. It turns away any feeling that might put a smile on my face or a spring in my step. Anger rains on everyone's parade. However, you can think of anger as a dukkha machine that you can control, and that you have the power to turn off. In fact, you can think of your power to switch off your dukkha machine as one of the most important skills you possess as a mature human being.

Journal Exercise 1-4: Turning Off Your Dukkha Machine

1. Write out a list of the excuses you use most often to justify letting yourself get angry. Don't evaluate or judge or condemn these excuses, but instead try to see how these excuses create a set of automatic choices that result in your losing your temper. What other choices could you make in these situations? Could you walk away until you've cooled off? Could you help solve the problem in some constructive fashion? Could you try to understand why this situation happened, so it won't happen again?

2. Write down four or five things you could start doing today that would help you refuse to be a mindless prisoner of your own anger. Let's assume that the world you live and work in isn't going to change all that much over the next year. This means that if your emotional climate is going to be any different, it is you who is going to have to change. Can you see any obvious places where you can make a start on this?

Rule 5: Be the Hero of Your Own Life Story

I've saved the best rule for last. It is time for you to realize that there are countless opportunities for extraordinary heroism in every new day of your life. It is heroic to do the following:

- Exercise self-control and live your life with dignity and compassion.

- Reduce the amount of suffering in this world.

- Give top priority to the well-being of others in every task you have to accomplish.

- Not berate and criticize someone who is wrong, whether that someone is your own kid, your spouse, your deeply annoying neighbor, or a store clerk having a bad day.

- Take charge of your own life.

- Stand up for someone who is being bullied.

- Offer your unconditional love to another human being.

- Make yourself vulnerable by accepting the love that someone else offers you.

- Be "right" and yet keep your mouth shut about it afterwards.

To control your anger you are going to have to become truly heroic. It is not enough to just suppress your angry feelings and impulses. Suppressing strong negative emotions will clog your arteries, which will lead you down a painful path to an early grave. What you have to do is to transform those strong negative feelings into strong positive actions.

Now, of course, it would be wonderful if reading this book would turn you into a perfect person—a living saint of some sort—but frankly that is not at all likely to happen. And I'm not trying to get you to turn yourself into some sort of inhumanly calm space cadet who takes no notice of what's going on in the world (there are plenty of medications on the market that will do that for you, if that is your ultimate wish).

I'm not suggesting that you try to do either of those things. Instead, I encourage you to be completely mindful of, concerned with, and even deeply passionate about your kids, your marriage, your extended family, and your friends. Pay attention to things like social injustice and wanton cruelty. Keep your kids from breaking your neighbor's windows, and care about how safe and pleasant the neighborhood is. Be heroic in your pursuit of these things.

Have you ever seen pictures of those brave little children and those courageous grandmothers who confronted the violent and angry race haters during the civil rights struggles in the 1960s? Do you remember Martin Luther King Jr.'s galvanizing force when he confronted the injustice of racial segregation in the United States? Have you ever heard what the Dalai Lama, the spiritual leader of Tibetan Buddhism, said when he was asked if he hated the Chinese, who had invaded his country and destroyed his people's culture? He answered, "The Chinese have stolen my country. I will not let them steal my heart." The deep message of the Dalai Lama, embraced by many who fought for civil rights in the last century, is that when a person provokes you to anger, you should look them in the eye and say, "Thank you. You have been my teacher."

Here is an idea you can store away to think about when you're lying in bed tonight: men's anger, their deep, abiding anger, is often rooted in shame, as Bill Pollack, respected Harvard researcher who studies the lives of boys, has described (1998). Pollack's observation is consistent with that of noted men's therapist Frank Pittman (1993), that men get angry because they fear that someone or something is making them look bad. Men lose their tempers because it distracts everyone, especially themselves, from noticing their weakness and their vulnerability. Anger is defensive and self-protective; it is never heroic. A hero is effective and courageous; a hero does not wallow in shame. He may be scared to death that his heroic actions are going to cost him his life, but it is overcoming the fear that makes him brave. It does not make him angry.

Being a hero also means not letting anyone steal your heart. It means transforming anger and rage into meaningful, directed, purposeful action. On an interpersonal level it means learning how to confront anger inside yourself and how to transform that anger into what psychologists call *assertiveness*. Through small and large acts of heroism you can not only become more aware of your anger but even transform it into a positive impulse that allows you to really look at and understand what is going on in the world around you. In the process, you can get yourself to a place where you can say to the people who seem to be trying to drive you right to the brink of insanity, "Thank you. You have been my teacher."

How could a person like you actively reduce the amount of suffering in the world every day? Well, you could discover a cure for cancer or implement a strategy to bring peace to the Middle East. Or you could simply make a focused and intentional effort to change the way you interact with everyone around you.

Journal Exercise 1-5: Being a Hero Means Acting Heroically

Think back on the suffering you have witnessed and maybe even have caused over the past few days. What could a hero like you have done to help reduce the quantity of that suffering? Write down everything you come up with, whether it is realistic or not. Explore your untapped potential for heroism. This is perhaps your first step toward developing that double consciousness mentioned earlier. You aren't just you in any given situation; you are also the potential hero of that situation. Practice thinking and acting heroically; record the results of your experience in your journal.

A CONCLUDING MEDITATION: MAKING ANGER DISAPPEAR

To inspire you and to encourage you, I offer some ideas distilled from the teachings of the Buddha (based on the Sangharakshita translation of Dhammapada, The Way of Truth, p. 423) and adapted from a translation by Robert Thurman (2005).

> Experiences are preceded by mind, led by mind, produced by mind. If one speaks or acts with an impure mind, suffering follows, even as the cart-wheel follows the hoof of the ox.

Experiences are preceded by mind, led by mind, produced by mind. If one speaks or acts with a pure mind, happiness follows, like a shadow that never departs.

Those who entertain such thoughts as "He abused me, he beat me, he defeated me, he robbed me" will not calm their anger.

Those who do not entertain such thoughts as "He abused me, he beat me, he defeated me, he robbed me" will calm their anger.

Here in the world, anger is never pacified by anger. It is pacified by love. This is the eternal truth. (vii)

Please accept this invitation to reflect mindfully on the meaning of these ancient words, and, when you are ready, write in your journal about what these words mean to you, based on your personal experience as a member of the human family.

2

Finding Your Center:
A Guide to Active
Self-Awareness

The fundamental idea you will encounter in this chapter is that just about everybody wants to be a good person. Being a good person is not always easy, but doing what you need to do to become a good person is about as natural a process as you can imagine. Because you were born a human being, your natural state in the world is to be connected with other people. Isolated, alienated, fearful, and angry people are living unnatural lives; they are out of sync with their deepest human nature. If you are convinced that all human beings are essentially selfish, rotten, and miserable, then you probably won't think this chapter makes much sense. But perhaps you will read it anyway, and open yourself up to a change of heart.

THE EXPERIENCE OF FLOW

The goal of this chapter is to get you moving toward recovering your human center—a place where you exist in harmony with yourself and with your fellow humans. Psychologists call this experience *flow* (Csikszentmihalyi 1990); it is a psychological state of being that exists when you are living your life with joy, creativity, and total involvement.

You experience flow when you are doing anything skillfully with complete attention and an open heart. Many men experience flow when they are engaged in physical activity—taking a long bike ride, playing tennis, or scoring the perfect goal. Flow can also be experienced while you are playing or listening to music, playing chess, or opening your heart completely to your partner when you are making love. You can experience flow when you are fishing with your kids or when you are praying. When you experience flow you may become aware that you are enjoying yourself so completely that nothing else really matters at that moment. You may become aware that physical pain no longer exists and that your entire being is invested in your immediate experience.

You disrupt flow when you become self-conscious, when you are messing up, when you feel the need to judge everything around you, and when you start worrying about how other people are responding to you. Anger is almost completely incompatible with any experience of flow. Anger hijacks your attention and your concentration, and it disrupts the smooth flow of your energy. *Optimal moments* do not occur when you are angry, since the anger narrows your awareness and constricts your heart—both biologically and metaphysically.

Living with an Open Heart

All healthy babies are born with a natural knowledge of what is good and important. Over the years as we have grown up we have all learned not to trust our hearts, and to various degrees we have turned away from our best and highest nature. When we stop trusting our instincts, we become concerned almost exclusively with self-protection. A closed heart spends most of its time avoiding feeling hurt, disappointed, and inferior. A closed heart comes to believe that other people can never be trusted, and that it is essential to uncover the bad intentions of other people. When this happens we close ourselves off from others, and we lose contact with what makes us human. That is why, in Buddhist teaching, anger is considered one of the greatest violations of human nature.

When our hearts close, we operate with neither flow nor self-awareness. Anger shuts off any meaningful contact with the core of the self, that part of you that in Buddhist teaching is called your Buddha nature.

Recovering Your Buddha Nature

Think back to the last time you experienced flow. Not only were you not angry, but you weren't even thinking about getting angry or keeping yourself from becoming angry. What were you doing when you had that experience?

Chances are you were well rested, thinking clearly, and actively engaged in what you were doing; you were probably not hungover. Interestingly, if you are like the vast majority of people who have reported on such moments in their lives, you were not watching television, doing anything particularly thrilling or dangerous, or even making a great deal of money. You were probably engaged in some activity that you take pride and pleasure in, and you were probably doing it because you had actively chosen to do it. Perhaps you were all by yourself, but you might well have been enjoying the company of a friend, your partner, or some members of your family. In the first exercise in this chapter, your goal is to come up with a short list of things you can remember doing in the recent past that brought you pleasure, fulfillment, and satisfaction.

Journal Exercise 2-1: Experiencing Flow

Your task in this exercise is to come up with about half a dozen ordinary events in your recent life when you experienced flow. Recall that *flow* is a psychological term for how a person feels when they are doing something they love, and doing it with grace and skill. These moments may occur while you are working, when you are enjoying a hobby, when you are doing something that you take real pride in, or when something unexpected and wonderful happens, such as a perfect sunrise that you happen to see or something really amazing that one of your kids does.

If you can, for each item on your list add a brief description of how you were feeling while this event took place. Can you figure out how you created the opportunity to have this very positive experience? You've experienced thousands of potentially perfect moments with your spouse, but you have probably been truly open to the possibility of a flow experience with her only a few times in the past year. What inside you created the possibility to be fully present, aware, and alive during the moments of flow that you actually experienced?

WHERE HAVE ALL THE FLOWERS GONE?

There was a time in our lives when our hearts were open, our dreams were unconstrained, and the future looked like something we couldn't wait to experience. We experienced the flow of first love, amazing athletic feats, the joy of best friendships. We had the energy to take on any task that captured our imagination.

What happened to us? When did our hearts begin to close, and how did we become so cynical and angry? What has become of our self-confidence and idealism? Where were we when the bright light of boyhood became the fluorescent glare of duty, responsibility, and unrewarding routine?

The sad fact is that I know very few men who are *not* angry. They may not walk around all the time with a chip on their shoulder, but they routinely overreact to perceived slights and deliberate or accidental insults. They are angry about their problems at work, the way the country is run, the way their computers lock up several times a day, and the fact that there is never enough money in their bank accounts after the bills are paid. Men are angry at the disrespect they encounter at every turn; they are angry at how much they are expected to conform. They are angered by injustice and indifference, and they are angered by how powerless they feel much of the time.

From a Buddhist perspective you might say that men are angered by the fact that so much has poisoned their hearts and clouded their self-awareness. Too many men literally can't remember the last time they laughed out loud or found the time to take their kids to the zoo; too many men can't remember the last time they actually made love or enjoyed the taste of a great meal. Their minds have become contaminated by the sorrows of everyday life. And they can't imagine an alternative to the way they lived yesterday, the day before yesterday, and the day, week, month, and year before that.

From a psychological perspective this loss of awareness can be traced back to boyhood. The way boys are raised sows the seeds that will be harvested when they are men. Because few men escape this fate, it makes sense to pay close attention to the roots of male anger, which lie in the way we treat boys and young men and how we prepare them to take their place in the world of men.

How to Raise a Depressed, Angry Boy

Therapists who work with depressed and angry men encounter the same cluster of psychological processes in the personality profiles of nearly all of their clients. It is pretty obvious that these men didn't come to be the way they are because of an unfortunate, disappointing experience or two. In fact, it is clear that by the time a young man enters high school his ways of processing information about himself and the world are already pretty well established. In depressed and angry men those ways only become more rigid (and largely irrational) as they enter manhood, unless they encounter mentors and role models who can show them a different way of thinking and being (Cochran and Rabinowitz 2000).

Below is a list of the six elements that psychologists have identified as the primary roots of men's anger and unhappiness.

Perfectionism. The golden rule for depressed and angry men is the doctrine of absolute perfectionism. Nowhere in all of psychology is there is a better-documented, more thoroughly validated, more emotionally crippling doctrine than the idea that a man has to do everything and constantly be perfect. Let's be clear: this does not fall into the category of such general encouragement as "Always do your best," "Any job that is worth doing is worth doing well," or other well-intentioned exhortations that you may have heard from non-pathological parents, teachers, and coaches. The sort of pathological perfectionism that I am pointing to is the kind that never rests, never lies still, and never, ever acknowledges a job done damned well, but with a little bit of imperfection. If you can't remember ever being praised or ever being able to measure up to what your dad considered to be "good enough," you may well have been raised in the Church of Unattainable Perfection.

Most of us are amateur perfectionists much of the time, but most of us don't routinely beat ourselves up over every imperfection we find. It's also true that when our computer software ties itself up in knots, when we allow ourselves to be transported in a gigantic aluminum tube at thirty-five thousand feet, we actually hope that the technical support people and the aircraft maintenance guys are at least a little more perfectionistic than the average guy down at the pool hall. We all pretty much cross our fingers in hope that our plumbers, surgeons, and tax return preparers are perfectionists. As you can see, I am not arguing that all perfectionism is bad, or that it isn't important to take pride in doing a job to the very best of one's ability. The real problem with the doctrine of absolute perfectionism is that it doesn't leave any room for growth, improvement, and optimism. Absolute perfectionism is deeply grounded in unrelenting self-criticism. An angry-young-man-in-training must be convinced, deep down, that nothing he has ever done, or ever will do, is good enough.

Unrelenting self-criticism. If you want to make any claim whatsoever to being a deeply angry man, you must 'fess up to having a really large reservoir of self-loathing and self-criticism. It is not enough that you are imperfect; what you must do is beat yourself up for your imperfections. And should anyone ever make the error of complimenting you on a job well done, you must immediately dismiss that person as a slacker, a fool, or both—an undiscerning, feckless nobody who doesn't have a right to an opinion about what you are doing. No young man can be considered a real man until he can put himself down with the best of them.

Unrelenting self-criticism is also essential to destroy and hopefully eliminate any potential self-esteem that a boy or a young man might start to develop on his road to manhood. The trend among young guys these days is to believe that the only thing that really matters is how muscular they are. The result has been an epidemic of *body dysmorphic disorder* (a pathological dislike and even rejection of one's own physical body or important features of one's body) among boys and young men, as described in the recent book *The Adonis Complex* by Harrison Pope and his colleagues (2000). Since it is virtually impossible for a teenager to be stronger than a grown man, and absolutely impossible to make himself taller or his penis larger, hating himself for being physically imperfect is a great strategy for turning frustrated and envious adolescent boys into angry, dissatisfied men. To make this even more complicated, many young men have decided to take a variety of performance-enhancing steroids—and long-term overexposure to these steroids is associated with anger control problems.

Self-blaming rumination. If you want to encourage your son to grow into an angry man, you must do everything in your power to nudge your boy toward a life of self-blaming rumination. This means he must never be taught or encouraged to just let things go. *He must go to his room and think about how deeply imperfect and flawed he is.* He should learn to brood like a real man. He should never joke about his shortcomings. He should punish himself over and over for his imperfections. He should be able to write a small book about how incomplete, unsuccessful, and disappointing he is as a human being. This kind of rumination is, after all, the linchpin of anger.

Rumination is what establishes the trip wires of powerful negative emotions in the human brain. Without rumination there could be virtually no self-condemnation, and in the absence of self-condemnation, self-acceptance would blossom, and who could imagine a depressed angry guy wallowing in a pool of soothing self-acceptance? Just to be on the safe side, insist that your son spend at least a couple of hours every day reflecting on what a miserable and unworthy person he is becoming.

No problem-solving skills. What a depressed and angry boy *ought* to feel is completely helpless and out of control. Don't distract him with thoughts about how things could be done better next time, or what can be learned from today's mistakes. Problem-solving leads to optimism, while obsessive and unhealthy rumination leads to acceptance of grim inevitabilities. When real angry men are at the top of their anger game you can't even suggest a compromise to them. As battered wives and abused children all over the world know, it is foolish and even dangerous to suggest an alternative strategy to a maddened man. If you catch your son in the act of being an optimistic, active problem solver you know that he is not taking his imperfections seriously!

A related idea that I run into all the time in my clinical work with young men is the belief that if they should ever stop beating up on themselves—if they should ever practice even a little bit of self-acceptance, if they should ever become active problem solvers as opposed to being vengeful self-punishers—they would suddenly become complete slackers. You have to wonder where this idea comes from. Who told your son that if he respected himself and honestly thought he could figure out how to do better he would be a failure as a man? As one young man told me recently, fighting back the tears that were filling his eyes, "I just can't let myself believe what you've been telling me. If I did I might let down my entire family and destroy my entire future." Who filled this wonderful young man's head with all that anger-making garbage? It wasn't me.

No self-awareness and no self-expression. Even if all of the preceding rules have been religiously followed, your son, or any other young man, could still find a way to escape becoming an angry and depressed man. He could have a therapist, a teacher, a coach, a minister, or a mom in whom he could confide and from whom he might seek solace. This must be discouraged at all costs. Self-awareness and self-expression (except, of course, for angry and/or violent displays of raw emotion) are not acceptable. Real (angry) men do not introspect. They do not talk about feelings. They never, ever express sadness, despair, or longing. They see other men solely as objects of competition. To them, there is something almost homosexual about a guy who can cry or ask for a hug. Concrete walls and alcohol are the only emotional outlets that angry young men need. If they have girlfriends, those relationships must be exclusively about sex, and the young women they have sex with should have the emotional depth of a Happy Meal. But you already knew that.

No self-acceptance. Finally, to make sure that the young man's heart is completely sealed off in a lead coffin, make sure that he learns to see the world as it really is. Make sure that he understands that the only, and I mean *only*, acceptance he can legitimately and appropriately recognize comes from other people. Specifically, the only acceptance that really counts is that which comes from other perfect men. Self-acceptance is a trap that can lead to a long and healthy life of playing with one's grandkids during a comfortable retirement while being surrounded by family and friends. Can you imagine anything more deluded?

Journal Exercise 2-2:
Depressed and Angry Habits Inventory

You've just read about the six common elements that define most angry men's childhoods. In this journal exercise, take a trip down memory lane and examine your own boyhood in light of what you learned about each of these six mental habits. Can you see the influence these habits have played in your education as an angry man? Take as much time and space as you need to really flush that stuff out of hiding. If you are feeling very brave about the whole thing, share your memories with your spouse, your kids, or a couple of guys you grew up with.

For each of the six problem habits, write as many recollections as you can come up with about the training you received as a boy and a young man.

Once you have completed this list, go back over it and underline the ones that have caused you the most trouble in your life. Take some time to reflect on how you can live your life just a bit differently in the future by bending or breaking some of the mental habits that have caused you the most pain.

Live Dangerously: Break Some Patterns

The interesting thing about these six habits is that you can *decide* to violate them one at a time or all at once, any time you wish. In fact, your pathway out of anger will become much clearer after you have begun to violate them in a deliberate and conscious way.

Begin with *perfectionism*. How can you begin the process of accepting imperfection in your world and yourself? You need to experience the uncomfortable feelings associated with your imperfections— the physical discomfort you will experience if you deliberately accept that you don't have to do everything perfectly. In fact, you might think about some of the fun and challenging things that you might try for the first time if you could get over your need to be perfect at everything you do. If you're feeling really courageous, ask your son or some other young person to teach you a skill, like skateboarding or playing the trumpet perhaps, that you know you are unlikely ever to fully master.

Self-criticism need not be a compulsion in your life. Try substituting some gentle self-deprecating humor the next time you want to beat yourself up. Try looking in the mirror and saying, "You know what? I really suck at a lot of things. I must be a normal human being."

Self-critical rumination is a tough nut to crack. Experiment with various ways of backing yourself out of a ruminating episode. Here are two suggestions that work for some people: (1) Slip a very sturdy elastic band around your wrist; then, every time you start ruminating on your failures, pull it back and give yourself a sharp slap on the wrist; and (2) every time you start to ruminate on the negative aspects of your life, immediately substitute a preplanned pleasant or funny thought—picture your boss naked, what it would feel like to drive your dream car, how it would feel to bowl a perfect game, and so on.

As for developing *problem-solving skills*, that's what this book is all about! The challenge is to be able to identify each new situation as a problem to be solved and not a test of your manhood, authority, and worth as a human being. This is a classic case of the need for practice, practice, practice.

When it comes to *self-awareness* and *self-expression*, you need to think not only about your verbal behavior (talking, confessing, shouting) but also about your nonverbal behavior as well. A mental disorder recently identified in men, called *alexithymia*, is described in detail in a good book on the psychology of men written by my friend Christopher Kilmartin (2000). *Alexithymia* is a fancy label for a guy's lack of awareness of the emotions he is currently experiencing. It's not clear whether these guys are really clueless about their feelings, or whether they just try as hard as they can to ignore the evidence. But one thing is for sure, alexithymia is rampant in angry and depressed men.

The "cure" for alexithymia is to learn how to find and say the words for what you are feeling or experiencing, especially when those feelings are strong and conflicted or confusing. Just picture the shock and bewilderment on the faces of your loved ones if you were to come out with a sentence like "You know, Sara, when you play your music that loud it makes me really tense and irritable, and that makes me realize that I'm close to losing my temper." Your wife or partner would probably think she'd died and gone to heaven if one day you just blurted out, "I'm feeling really on edge right now. You know what would feel really great? A big hug." Try it. It sounds impossible, but it can be done!

For ways to break the *self-acceptance* edict, read on.

Journal Exercise 2-3:
Making Some New Resolutions

Most likely, the people who taught you all those bad mental habits that have messed up your life aren't part of your day-to-day life anymore. And your conformity to their rules is likely interfering in a serious way with your most important current relationships. If you were smart enough to learn all those rules when you were a kid, you are probably smart enough to be able to unlearn those rules as an adult. So the task for you now is to decide to create some new resolutions that will take your life in a different direction.

The point of these resolutions should be to counteract a lot of your old, worn-out masculinity training and increase your awareness of your own feelings and thought processes, and of how you are influencing the people around you. Start with trying to internalize three simple new resolutions: (1) to become more aware of your emotional response to frustration and disappointment; you might call this the Real Men Get Over It rule; (2) to become more aware of other people's distress; it could be called the Good Men Care About Other People resolution; and (3) to see beyond the present moment; perhaps this could be called the Mature Men Realize That They Will Laugh About This Tomorrow resolution.

In your journal, record your experience of trying to live consistently by these three resolutions over the next few days and weeks.

A BUDDHIST PERSPECTIVE ON ANGER

Of course, it's worthwhile to think about all these unfortunate mental habits that mess up men's lives. But since Buddhism doesn't grant the luxury of dismissing angry men as simply a bunch of ignorant, hot-headed, immature, narcissistic, spoiled jerks, we also need to develop a somewhat deeper level of philosophical analysis of anger if we are to really understand the problems that angry men live with. It is a fundamental assumption in Buddhism that angry people are not bad people. From a compassionate perspective, we can see angry people as lost and confused, but not bad or different from other people. In Buddhist philosophy a lost being is considered a wasted being, and the Buddha was adamant that no being should ever be wasted. So we need to look more carefully at the question of getting to know our angry selves more deeply. To accomplish this quantum leap in self-awareness we need to address the one inevitable fact of everyone's existence: that we are going to die.

Coming to Terms with Your Own Mortality

Did you ever pause to wonder what your family, neighbors, and coworkers will make of your life after you are gone? Do you have any idea what your real legacy will be on this planet after your heirs have spent the last of their inheritance on Caribbean cruises and cosmetic surgery? Have you ever wondered if the life you have lived thus far means anything at all?

It's time to apply some ancient Greek wisdom to your own miserable existence. That wisdom states that the quality of a man's life cannot be truly judged until it is known how he died. Prepare yourself, my friend; it is time to take stock of your final moments on Spaceship Earth.

Journal Exercise 2-4: Writing Your Obituary

Your task is to engage in a mindful thought experiment in which you realize that today could be the very last day of your life. Given this forewarning of the end, it is now time for you, just as we all must, to take stock and consider where you are at this point in your life, in these final hours before your demise.

The point of this exercise is for you to understand that a human life—your life—is something that has to be accounted for in the immediate moment, not in some distant future. Take this opportunity to examine the complete measure of your own mortal experience as if you were about to draw your last breath at any moment.

So, please put down this book now, fire up your computer or get out your journal, and start writing. The title of your essay will be your name, followed by your birth date, and then today's date. Write it from the perspective of a close friend who knew you well. Go ahead and make it as melodramatic as you want. But wait! There's one more thing! Unlike most people's obituaries, your obituary must be brutally honest, frank, and revealing—a reasonably accurate assessment of your life as you have lived it up until today. Here's an example of what it should look like:

Wally Q. Citizen
May 24, 1956–October 23, 2005

Wally Citizen was found dead today sitting in front of his home computer. He was in the process of writing an angry letter to the mayor about the neighborhood kids playing street hockey in front of his house. He was forty-nine years old. The cause of death was his heart, which had shrunk and hardened until it broke into a thousand pieces. He died alone, and very few people evidently cared. Wally is survived by his wife, Beth, who described Wally as a hard man to live with, and certainly not the loving, kind, and funny man she had fallen in love with so many years before, when Jimmy Carter was president. She will be unable to attend the funeral due to a long-scheduled hair appointment. Wally is also survived by his three grown children, who are trying to raise their own children to be as different from their grandfather as possible, but who are now looking forward to having a close relationship with their mother, which was impossible while Wally was alive. Wally was a long-term employee of the Ace Corporation, whose representative described Wally as honest, reliable, dependable, and the source of more human unpleasantness than any ordinary working person ever ought to be subjected to just to feed her family. Wally is remembered by his three surviving friends as a guy who knew he was always right. One of them commented, "Now that Wally is gone, I suppose the world will go to hell in a handbasket. I wonder if he's already telling the Lord how to manage things in heaven." No flowers, no regrets; life will pretty much go on as usual. May he rest in peace (at long last).

ANALYZING YOUR OBITUARY

When you take a look at your obituary, you will probably notice a few things about your sad story. First, it is pretty realistic in at least one sense: Anger kills. For reasons that will be explained in the next chapter, chronic anger is directly responsible for a variety of serious health problems, including heart attacks and strokes. Angry guys rarely live very long after they retire—if they even make it that far. Angry guys also die of alcohol-related illnesses and accidents at a much greater rate than their more laid-back peers; and of course angry guys are also more likely to die in accidents that are caused by or related to their tempers. (Things really don't go so well when one pissed-off guy gets into a traffic accident with another pissed-off guy—especially if one of them is packing a weapon.)

Second, you'll probably notice that your obituary is somewhat overly pessimistic. Actually, Beth probably will go to Wally's funeral, and the kids will probably go too. Nobody is really going to be all that glad that Wally is in the ground, although they might feel a tiny bit of relief. But of course Wally imagines that people won't spend a lot of time crying when they get the bad news of his passing; a prime reason for Wally's pessimism is that he's been doggedly following all those wretched, self-defeating requirements we went over earlier in this chapter.

Below we'll take a look at several of the emotionally harmful mistakes that depressed and angry people commonly make when they talk or write about themselves. See how many of them you included in your obituary exercise.

Negative self-statements—the garbage within. When unhappy folks find themselves in anger-arousing situations they generate a whole lot of *negative self-statements* (Dua and Swinden 1992). When research psychologists put angry people and regular people in situations where they are deliberately provoked to anger, both the regular people and the chronically angry people tend to get pretty cranky. But only the angry people characteristically turn that anger toward themselves as well as toward the people who happen to be around them. What is really happening is that the episode triggers a barrage of negative and hostile thinking—and a whole lot of it ends up attaching itself to thoughts that angry people are having about themselves and the world.

Here's a sample of the kinds of thoughts that researchers recorded when they asked people with a history of anger problems to tell them what was going through their minds during the incident (Harmon-Jones 2004):

- "I am no damned good."

- "I have *never* been any damned good."

- "I am useless and helpless."

- "I have no ability to control this or any other situation."

- "The worst possible things always happen to me."

- "Life is never going to get any better."

- "This situation is going to end in disaster."

Psychologists have also noted two really important things about these angry, self-destructive thoughts and ideas. The first is that when the angry people are not being provoked, when their lives and minds are in neutral, they know perfectly well that all these statements are a moldering heap of donkey dung.

Second, and more important, these thoughts have a nasty way of becoming self-fulfilling prophecies. What happens is that you begin to act toward yourself and others *as if* these donkey-dung thoughts and impulses were true. You then begin to assume that other people also believe these things about you!

So now you are pissed off at the situation, at yourself, and at all those jerks out there who believe . . .

- *You* are no damned good.

- *You* have *never* been any damned good.

- *You* are useless and helpless.

- *You* have no ability to control this or any other situation.

- The worst possible things are targeted right at *you.*

- *Your* life is never going to get any better.

- *Your* situation is going to end in disaster, unless *you* have a heart attack first.

Projections—the drama in your own head. Psychologists call thoughts and feelings like these *projections,* and angry people are projecting fools. They "see" evidence of other people's malignant thoughts and impulses all around them every day. Of course, they are making 90 percent of it up, but they have the God-given right to believe every word and impulse of it. No wonder they are so angry all the time—just look at what all those other people are thinking about them! Not until they get into therapy (if then) do they become even marginally aware that all these critical thoughts and judgments are actually coming from inside their own heads. The fact is that if you could calm yourself down you'd realize that most people aren't even paying that much attention to you, let alone wasting their energy trying to make you lose your temper.

There's a quick and easy way to see if I'm right about this. Right now, go back and reread your obituary. Underline every bit of self-defeating garbage, especially the self-defeating garbage that you have projected on others. Can you see evidence that this self-downing projection is whirring away somewhere inside that crooked brain of yours?

Anger's Connection with Depression

Especially in men, anger and depression are biologically and psychologically almost the same thing. Remember all those rotten things they believe about themselves when they are provoked to anger? Well, eventually, angry men start to believe those things all the time, even when they're not provoked. Often, therapists working with depressed angry men can't draw a line between where the anger ends and the depression begins, or vice versa. As Phillip Martin observed in his 1999 book, *The Zen Path Through Depression*, when we are ill with depression we are literally sick with anger.

Although it might seem pretty obvious that self-downing thoughts experienced in a moment of anger are just products of the moment and not really true, after a while, if you go through this process several times a week, the crazy thoughts start to have a ring a truth about them. You begin to wonder, at least at some unconscious level, if there might not be something to the idea that you are no damned good. How many times can a person call himself a stupid son of a bitch before the idea begins to take on a life of its own? If you do this consistently enough, you will almost certainly end up with a well-deserved diagnosis of clinical depression.

The self-defeating processes that go on in the hearts and minds of angry folks are a whole lot more complicated and significant than plain old-fashioned feeling sorry for yourself. People who are feeling sorry for themselves are probably kind of keeping one eye out for some source of tea and sympathy while they are throwing their little pity parties. But angry folks more or less have both eyes wide open—and they drive themselves (and others) crazy with their unrelenting quest to challenge all those people who might be critical of them, and who might even agree that they are no damned good ("They say I'm helpless? Ineffective? Powerless? Worthless? Well, by God, I'll show them!"). And this quest very quickly becomes an emotional and mental roller coaster that it is almost impossible to climb down from.

A CONCLUDING MEDITATION: MINDFULNESS

In Buddhist thought, the angry mind is considered a contaminated mind. A contaminated mind corrupts the body (as we will see in detail in chapter 3), starves the true self, and destroys human relationships. This contamination is a combination of anger, greed, and delusion. Each of these is inextricably linked to the others, and each has to be addressed before you can go significantly farther. Anger is the seedbed for depression because angry men commit two great sins against their true human nature: they avoid human contact and they do not seek support. They neglect and abandon their Buddha nature, their true self.

But how does one find and restore connection with this true self? Where is a man's true human center? This is where the practice of mindfulness begins to come to our attention. Nobody can tell someone else how to do this; each and every person has to find it and experience it in his or her own way. Fortunately, the directions that explain how to accomplish this are completely accessible to every human being on the planet.

Thus, this chapter concludes with a meditation, something for you to think about, reflect upon, and search for truth within. After you have read the passage below (written by Jon Kabat-Zinn [1994], the West's leading proponent of mindfulness, in his wonderful book *Wherever You Go There You Are*), spend some time thinking deeply about what it means. When you are ready, record your thoughts and reflections about this passage in your journal.

Try watching your reactions in situations that annoy you or make you angry. Notice how even speaking of something "making" you angry surrenders your power to others. Such occasions are good opportunities to experiment with mindfulness [paying close attention to what is going on inside your own head and heart] as a pot into which you can put all your feelings and just be with them, letting them slowly cook, reminding yourself that you don't have to do anything with them right away, that they will become more cooked, more easily digested and understood simply by holding them in the pot of mindfulness.

Observe the ways in which your feelings are creations of your mind's view of things, and maybe that view is not complete. Can you allow this state of affairs to be okay and neither make yourself right or wrong? Can you be patient enough and courageous enough to explore putting stronger and stronger emotions into the pot and just holding them and letting them cook, rather than projecting them outward and forcing the world as you want it to be now? Can you see how this practice might lead to knowing yourself in new ways, and freeing yourself from old, worn-out limiting views? (245–46)

3

Paying Attention
to Your Body

Anger is a complicated and serious biological event. In this chapter you will learn some important skills for becoming aware of and exercising greater control over the way your body reacts to stress. Most people are unaware of the extent to which their moods and their ways of dealing with the world are influenced by their physiology. In practicing mindfulness you will not only become much more aware of what your body is doing but also learn how to control your moods and interpersonal behavior, by exercising conscious control of your blood pressure, your heart rate, and your entire autonomic nervous system.

ANGRY MEN DROP DEAD

No, this isn't a command! It's a simple statement of fact. Anger releases a cascade of hormones in your body that activate a series of circuits in your brain, which make you unable to think clearly and which command your muscles, organs, and digestive processes to quit what they are doing and prepare to go to war. When your body does this repeatedly you become physically and emotionally exhausted. And, when you continue to repeat this process while in a state of exhaustion, you start doing serious damage to yourself. Do it long enough and you will die.

Anger literally kills men. It does it in three main ways. First, it destroys their cardiovascular system. Second, it wrecks their immune system; and third, it effectively blocks the most important natural system that helps them recover from prolonged or excessive periods of hyperarousal (Hogan and Linden 2004; Richards, Alvarenga, and Hof 2000; Sapolsky 1998, 2004). I'll talk more about that third system later in the chapter.

The View from Your Brain

In the last chapter we examined the experience of flow. When you are in flow you are actually using your brain in the way that nature intended. If you could somehow stick your brain in a gigantic neural imaging machine when you're experiencing flow, you would see that the neural connections in the right frontal lobes of your brain are all happily glowing with activity. At the same time, the visual parts of your brain are busily sending signals to all of the other brain centers, keeping your actions well coordinated, and helping you accurately anticipate what is going to happen next. All those painful years of evolution have paid off, just as nature intended, and you truly are the most magnificent creature in all of creation.

The reason this is so important is that it shows that you aren't brain damaged! You may not be using your brain very successfully or happily much of the time, but if you can still lose yourself in a good game of chess, or in growing a perfect tomato, or in holding up your part in the all-guys kazoo orchestra, then we know that your brain is still capable of functioning in wonderful ways.

On the other hand, when you are angry, the lights literally go out in your right frontal lobe (Harmon-Jones 2004). The left frontal lobe takes over, and it is connected to the parts of your brain that are much less developed—for anything other than fighting for survival. Those visual centers start to go dark. Your optimism vanishes as if someone has just flipped a switch, which in some sense is exactly what your brain has done. You may now be fully ready to defend yourself and fight your way out of a trap, but you have sacrificed almost all of your mental flexibility, your sense of humor, and your ability to change your mental channel. Should a psychologist suddenly ask you to take a test of your mental agility at this moment, you would do very poorly on that test. Your thinking would be rigid, absolutist, full of logical errors, and unable to discern subtle changes going on in the world around you. Your problem-solving skills would resemble those of a donkey; and you would not be able to remember a damned thing about anything you've learned so far in this book.

Anger and Depression

Chronic anger is highly correlated with a variety of biological changes that can come to feel perfectly normal—except that over time they will cause a person's physical body to fall apart. Mother Nature has very strong views about how a human life is to be lived, and she exacts a high price for not paying attention to her basic requirements.

As noted in the previous chapter, psychologists have long recognized the powerful connection between depression and anger (Troisi and D'Argenio 2004). That connection is even obvious in the psychobiology of angry people—their brains and cardiovascular systems are virtually indistinguishable from those of chronically depressed people. This observation has led a number of therapists to argue that the way we usually think about depression as a psychological syndrome actually often leads to missed diagnoses in depressed men. This is because, although their biological profiles may be amazingly similar, the way that depressed women and men interact with the world around them appears to be so different.

The common denominator in both cases is that there is (1) a profound disruption in the brain's processing of information, (2) a high level of dangerous stress hormones in the brain and the cardiovascular system, and (3) abandonment of pleasure in favor of a rigid and inflexible way of interacting with the world. In both depression and anger, what is lost is a person's ability to successfully negotiate the social and emotional complexities of everyday life. As the ability to navigate one's life becomes corrupted, the ability to know and experience an adaptive self begins to deteriorate. When a person is no longer confident in the integrity of his self, he no longer has a reliable base from which he can confront and solve problems. In other words, his life (along with his physical well-being) begins to fall apart. It's no surprise, then, that chronic depression, like chronic anger, strongly correlates with the incidence of coronary heart disease.

How to Give Yourself a Heart Attack

Cardiovascular disease is the number one killer in the United States (Benson 1975; Sapolsky 2004) and the entire industrialized world. You can probably blame the ridiculously slow course of human evolution for this problem. What we have done is taken a biological machine that was designed for self-defense on a sparsely populated savannah and transported it to a modern world where your competition is no longer a hungry lion lying in wait by the watering hole. Instead, it's a guy talking on his cell phone while mindlessly driving four thousand pounds of steel down the freeway at eighty miles an hour.

The lion was pretty tough competition, but evolution endowed you with a big brain, so you were able to learn her habits. You could calculate what time is safest to take your kids out to play, and when to forage for a tasty tuber or a bit of leftover wildebeest. Once you had the lion pretty much figured out, you could afford to let down your guard, tell a few jokes, take a nap, enjoy some mutual grooming with a mate, or learn a new magic trick. While you were doing these things, your brain was sending signals to your body that it was time to repair some of the wear and tear you incurred the last time you had to run like hell to escape becoming the lion's dinner. Your biology was well designed for this kind of intermittent but sometimes very high stress. Besides, your life expectancy wasn't all that great—so the system only had to be pretty good, and it didn't have to accommodate any long-term costs.

Unlike the lion on the savannah, the guy on the cell phone is a constant danger to you. There is no way for you to tell when he is going to decide to suddenly swerve his SUV into your lane and slam on his brakes. At work you can't afford to ask somebody in the next cubicle if they'd like to check your scalp for lice or join you for a nap in the shade. You can't take a half hour off to wrestle with your kids or make love to your partner. You have to be on the job literally forty, fifty, or sixty hours a week, and then there's the commute, the mortgage, the idiots who run the government, the computer that claims that you bought airplane tickets to Tibet, and the coach of your son's Little League team who does everything exactly the wrong way. All this, and you also happen to want to live to a ripe old age.

Now, you are asking your cardiovascular system to do a job it simply wasn't designed to do. Your system is cranking out cholesterol at a killing rate—because that is what it is designed to do when you are under stress—and that cholesterol is piling up in the form of plaque in your arteries, causing your blood pressure to creep upward. Since the wildebeest restaurant has been closed for several thousand years, you sit at your desk and eat high-cholesterol food designed for teenagers—gaining a few more pounds to make sure that your heart has to work even harder—and try to suppress the urge to kill when your boss sends you an e-mail saying that the project you have been working on has to be scrapped due to a decision made by the golf-playing idiots in the executive offices.

Of course, you don't have time to exercise, and even if you could make the time you are so physically tired that you can't imagine going to all the trouble anyway. You rarely sleep well; you either have trouble falling asleep or you wake up way too early. So you ruminate on all the crappy things that are wrong in your life, and by the time you arrive home, to be honest, nobody is all that excited to see you.

The end result of all this stress is that, biologically speaking, you are an accident waiting to happen. In fact, if on the way home you encounter a potential trigger for a major anger episode (that jerk with the cell phone swerves into your lane, you recall that conversation with your boss, or you find yourself thinking about what an idiot your kid's soccer coach is), your risk of having a heart attack will double over the next two hours.

Lethal Hostility

Believe it or not, at this point things are still not as bad as they could be. To really raise your risk of having a heart attack or a stroke you need to add an attitudinal component to your witch's brew of stress hormones, cholesterol, and arterial plaque. That emotional component is *hostility*.

A number of years ago health researchers began a series of what are called *prospective studies* of people in high-stress occupations. In a prospective study, researchers measure just about every meaningful variable they can find in a group of at-risk people, and then they wait to see who will live and who will not.

Graduate and professional schools are great places to start such a study. Graduate schools are full of ambitious, frustrated, stressed-out perfectionists who rarely take care of themselves physically or emotionally. They are the most competitive and hard-driving characters you'll ever meet, and their intelligence makes them excellent research subjects. Generally speaking, graduate students are also poor enough that you can get them to volunteer for a study for the price of a pizza, and, unlike your kids, they are trained not to complain.

Well, it turns out, if you want to determine who is a likely candidate for heart attack, stroke, and premature death, you won't be all that successful if you just measure things like perfectionism, sleep deprivation, heart rhythms, cholesterol levels, and stress hormones. These variables are important, of course, but the predictor that really makes a difference is a purely psychological one: hostility is the real killer. In fact, if you could know only one factor, and you wanted to predict who would end up in an early grave, the one factor you should examine is how angry a young professional is when he (or she) is in his (or her) mid-twenties (Smith and Houston 1987; Suarez and Williams 1989). The fact is that among those preprofessional and graduate students, 20 to 25 percent of them will not live to see their fiftieth birthday.

Hostility: Suppression Is Not the Answer

Now that you know how dangerous anger, especially hostility, is to your health, it will be tempting to try to hide your anger so you can avoid having to think about how unhealthy it is for you to lose your temper.

Unfortunately, if you try to suppress your anger, you will end up in even worse shape than you were in before you started reading this chapter. The result will be a veritable storm of glucocorticoids (these are steroid hormones released by the adrenal glands and are the building blocks of stress-based diseases) in your sympathetic nervous system, and a dramatic increase in your blood pressure and heart rate. Heart attack, here we come.

Hostility in the city. There is some evidence indicating that even living around hostile people can be bad for your health. People who live in cities where the ambient level of hostility is high (think Philadelphia, New York, and Chicago) have higher rates of cardiovascular disease than their peers in more laid-back cities. Naturally, people in these high-stress cities are also more likely to smoke, be overweight, eat poorly, and drink too much, but anger is the factor that puts them over the edge. All you have to do is take a cab ride in a high-hostility town if you want to see how persistently and pervasively anger is expressed in response to the everyday stresses of getting from place to place.

A while back, the *New York Times* ran a short news article that highlighted just how unexpected a nonhostile and non-stress-provoking approach in an urban environment can be. The article reported that an executive had left his hotel and gotten into a cab, headed for a very important meeting. The cab driver said he knew a shortcut across town and took his passenger down a series of narrow alleys that avoided the congestion of midtown Manhattan. Halfway down one alley, the cabbie found himself behind a city garbage truck whose crew was loading a huge mountain of trash—and doing so rather slowly. The cab driver, exercising the hostility that seems to come naturally to New York cab drivers, began blasting his horn, which accomplished very little except to upset his passenger and the sanitation workers, who now staged a slowdown. The cab driver began to back up, but he was blocked almost immediately by two other cabs that had come down the same alley. Now they were all equally stuck and the newcomers quickly joined in the blasting of horns.

Here's where the story gets interesting. The business man calmly removed his coat, got out of the cab, and started helping load the trash into the garbage truck!

No wonder the story made it into the *Times*! This guy might live forever.

Repressing or suppressing anger (or any other strong emotion) is very bad medicine indeed (Gross and Levenson 1993). And, in a research study, those early-death young professionals we talked about a little earlier were shown most likely to get sick and die if they made major efforts to hold all their negative emotions in check. Their colleagues who managed to stay alive past age fifty were just as hostile and angry, but they tended to give full expression to their feelings. The emotion suppressors were the ones who dropped dead in middle age (Smith and Houston 1987; Suarez and Williams 1989).

So this presents a bit of a dilemma. If you are a hostile, angry person who wants to stay alive, then you should express all that nastiness for the whole world to see. But how incredibly unpleasant that would be. And how depressing it would be to realize that the biggest prick in your office is likely to outlive you. Once again, I suppose you have to blame evolution. The great raging alpha-male cave dwellers probably lived longer than their victims. Back in those days, if you could stay on top with bluster, temper, and shows of aggression you would probably get the best stuff to eat, the safest places to sleep, and the most sex. So what if people hated you; you'd survive, and that is all that evolution really cares about. However, if you are reading this book, chances are that you're looking for a better way.

Your Immune System: The Bad News and the Good News

Chronic anger and stress will also play hell with your body's immune system. Stress is a serious problem for people with auto-immune diseases like rheumatoid arthritis, peptic ulcers, multiple sclerosis, diabetes, and latent viruses such as herpes and HIV. Angry people are more prone to getting colds and flu, and even infections from cuts and skin abrasions. The immune system response is affected by the intensity of a person's stressors, the duration and frequency of the stressors, and the degree to which a person can exercise control over those stressors.

THE BAD NEWS: STRESS AND YOUR IMMUNE SYSTEM

Psychologists have long observed that when people are confronting stress the things they do in order to feel better actually make them feel worse. Consuming alcohol certainly fits this pattern, as does eating lots of junk food, and not getting enough sleep. Paradoxically, the best ways of boosting your immune system during a period of stress are probably the very last things that you are likely to do. Making sure that you are eating a well-balanced diet on a regular schedule is one of those things. Getting some exercise, getting some sunshine and fresh air, changing your work routine, and making sure that you get a good night's sleep are all important activities to keep your immune system up to snuff. And it's hard to do any of those things when you are all wrapped up in a rage or plotting your revenge against somebody who has significantly contributed to your stress levels.

In the fascinating world of *psychoneuroimmunology* (the study of how your emotional system affects your immune system), stress is seen as the common denominator in just about every disease you can imagine. Cancerous tumors grow faster in animals that are stressed. Children who are chronically stressed don't grow to be as big as other kids. Soldiers who experience combat often develop post-traumatic stress disorder, and cancer patients subjected to chronic stress are less able to tolerate their treatments. Stress negatively affects people with chronic allergies as well as college students, many of whom spend the first few days after their final exams sick in bed.

THE GOOD NEWS:
THE IMPORTANCE OF PHYSICAL EXERCISE

There are two important things anyone can do to improve their *immunocompetence* (the body's ability to fight off infection and disease). Moreover, because anger is a major source of the stress that attacks our immune systems, it turns out that both of these important steps can play an important part in your comprehensive program of anger reduction. Both of these immune system boosters are really basic, but both are quite likely to be ignored or pushed aside in the press of our day-to-day lives. The first is paying attention to the wellness of our physical bodies, and the second is maintaining our connections with other people.

A program of regular physical aerobic exercise is a great way to begin boosting your immune system. It has been known for many years that working out on a regular basis, for at least thirty minutes three or more times a week, has a greater antidepressant effect than any pharmaceutical on the market. Exercise is also the single best way to promote cardiovascular health and stop the mental processes that generate and maintain anger. There's also evidence that regular aerobic exercise is good for your self-esteem, your weight, and your ability to get a good night's sleep.

Exercise is important even if you are overweight, eat bad food, smoke, and generally abuse your physical being. But of course exercise is even more effective if you are much more careful about what you eat, try to lose a few pounds, and stop smoking. It is probably almost impossible to do all these things at once, but they all sort of go together in an overall wellness plan. So make a decision to try some of this out, and begin to show the world that you really do have some self-respect. Working out, losing weight, and quitting smoking will almost certainly give a major boost to your self-esteem (there is a real link between self-esteem and becoming less angry). Give it a try. The exercise below may help you get and stay on track.

Journal Exercise 3-1: Focus on Wellness

Taking care of your physical being is an essential part of your anger control program, because it reduces your stress level, increases your feeling of optimism, and helps you feel better about yourself and the world in general. In this exercise you'll focus on getting a moderate amount of regularly scheduled exercise to improve your overall health and well-being.

1. Consult with a personal trainer or your doctor to develop a safe and healthy program of aerobic exercise that is appropriate for your age, weight, general health, and weekly schedule.

2. If you can, recruit a buddy to work out with you—someone who will keep you honest, provide you with a bit of healthy competition, and give you some company as you work on your physical well-being.

3. In your journal, write down the components of your exercise program and your fitness goals that you aim to achieve. Keep a record of how faithful you are at keeping up your intentions.

TAKING CONTROL OF YOUR BODY

In mindfulness the goal is to get off the stress-illness roller coaster. Here's the way-out-there, radical, new-age assumption we're working on: *the body and the mind have to learn to work together.* Actually, despite several hundred years of Western philosophy that actively and aggressively discouraged us from understanding it, this isn't a very complicated concept.

As a baby, when you were hungry and wet, you got upset, you fretted, you cried, and you got fed. With a full tummy and a clean diaper, your autonomic arousal system went into reverse, and you had a nice nap. Your arousal and your mood were correlated. It was only later, when the frontal lobes in your brain began to develop more fully, that you began to worry about whether mom and dad would always be there when you needed something. One day you were playing blissfully with Mr. Bunny, and the next day you couldn't find him, which made you feel distressed. Okay, so you developed a little of what developmental psychologists call *object permanence,* but you thereby stepped into a whole world of worry and uncertainty.

This new world of distress didn't have anything to do with an empty stomach and a full diaper; it was all about a whole bunch of abstractions, like being good at sports and getting the approval of your friends. You experienced anger, and even rage. You became apprehensive and worried, and then at puberty testosterone flooded your brain and you figured out that beating the crap out of something was one way to express those confusing bad feelings. From then on your head and your heart were often at cross-purposes. Making sense out of what you were feeling became a constantly increasing challenge. Your body tried to gain control of your mind while your mind was often at odds with your gut. The safest route was to shut down the "feelings" system and go with the biological agenda—with all this arousal going on inside, there had to be a hungry lion out there somewhere!

The truth is that now, by this point in your adult life, both your body and your mind are more or less on automatic pilot, and they aren't communicating with each other very well either. The biggest and most important question today is how to restore equilibrium, how to reassert control over both of those monkeys without taking the easy way out and hammering them both into submission with alcohol or some fancy antidepressant.

In the first two chapters we looked at some ways to reassert mental, cognitive, or intellectual control over this process, with the idea that you can start thinking about yourself and your world differently, and that this will, over time, get you to behave differently and intentionally. Eventually your nervous system will get on board with the program, and you'll be able to live your life as a healthy and rational human being.

And that will happen, if you live long enough and try hard enough. But a better solution is to also open a second front in the struggle to reassert control over your life. That second front is going to focus on your physical well-being. The goal is to have your physical self join forces with your mental self in order to generate and stabilize change in how you interact with the world. You've already started exercising on a regular basis, and that's a great start. Read on to find out how to martial your forces to establish this second front.

The Body Scan and the Relaxation Response

Let's talk about two exercises that, if you practice them on a regular basis, will start you back on the road toward longevity and physical well-being. The first exercise is called a *body scan*, and its purpose is simply to reintroduce you to your own body. This is really a form of meditation, because by doing this exercise you will actually be retraining your mind to pay attention to what is happening inside the envelope of your skin. This exercise should take you between twenty and thirty minutes, and you should try to do it once or twice a day. The second exercise is called the *relaxation response*. It is an excellent way to reduce the physical stress that we carry around in our muscles, and it is also a superb technique for regaining emotional equilibrium in emotionally challenging situations.

THE BODY SCAN

The goal of the body scan is to help you become fully aware of what your body is doing in the here and now. Begin this exercise by finding a comfortable place to sit or lie down. If you want to sit, select a chair that supports your back and allows you to have both feet on the floor (not a recliner). If you want to lie down, use a gym mat or a yoga mat if possible. It's probably not a good idea to use a bed, since you want to keep your mind fully alert during this exercise.

Make sure you're wearing comfortable clothes, and remove your shoes. If you can, find a place where the light is natural and the ambient sound is not intrusive. Turn off your cell phone, and make sure that the TV isn't on. If you want to work on this exercise while sitting at your desk, put a pleasant scene or a neutral screen saver on your computer monitor. You can play some relaxing music, but most people prefer either ordinary room noise or sound-deadening earphones. If you are a very time-conscious person, set a timer for thirty minutes, but then turn the timer away from you so you won't be worrying about how much time is left.

1. Close your eyes, or leave them half open, whichever is more comfortable for you.

2. Begin the exercise by taking several deep, full breaths through your nose. See if you can count to ten during both the in breath and the out breath. This will take some practice at first. Your breathing should come from your abdomen—that is, you should draw your breath in and push your breath out by using the muscles of your diaphragm. For some people, just practicing this part of the exercise is a full workout for the first few sessions. In fact, you could spend the rest of your life practicing to become a Zen master, and you might never do anything more complicated than learning how to pay attention to your breath!

3. As you continue to breathe slowly and regularly, turn your attention to your left foot. Notice any feelings or sensations in your toes, the ball of your foot, the bottom of your foot, the instep, your heel, the top of your foot, and now your left foot as a whole. You are not supposed to *do* anything with or about anything you experience. If you feel an ache or an itch, your job is to take note of that feeling and then move on to the next part. You'll probably be amused and amazed at how noisy your foot is. There are all those muscles and bones and joints and tendons, and all that skin—and once your foot figures out that you are actually paying attention to it for once, it will just start chattering

away. That's perfectly natural, and actually it is also pretty funny. There's something wonderful and strange about being encased in a sack of skin full of nerve endings.

4. Keep your attention there as long as you like, but eventually shift your attention from your left foot to your left ankle, shin, and lower leg. Pay attention to each part just as you did when you paid attention to your foot.

5. Now move your attention up to your knee, your upper leg, and your left thigh. Once you have gotten to your hip, cast your attention down to the foot again and rescan everything on your left side from the tip of your big toe to the big bones of your left hip. Then start the process all over again with the right foot, ending with your right hip. When you have finished that process, rescan your entire lower right side.

6. After making sure that your breathing is still slow and regulated, extend your body scan to your left hand, focusing on the fingers, palm, and skin. Then move to your left wrist, left forearm, elbow, and all the muscle groups in your upper arm. Scan your left arm as a whole, and then repeat this sequence with your right hand and arm.

7. Turn your attention now to your hips, and scan your lower back and belly. Even if you haven't experienced anything very strong up until now, you are sure to find some interesting sensations emanating from this region.

8. Next, scan your tailbone and your butt. Pay attention to your genitals; see how they are feeling today, and make sure they don't feel left out. Scan the area around your navel and then scan up the sides of your torso around your kidneys.

9. Continue scanning your chest, shoulders, and upper back. Now you should be able to scan your entire body, from the tips of your toes to your shoulders, paying close attention to what every part of your body is feeling and experiencing.

10. Finally, scan your neck, your jaw muscles, the inside of your mouth (tongue, gums, and teeth), your facial muscles, the

muscles around your eyes, your scalp around your ears, and the back of your head. Then scan the muscles in your forehead and your scalp on top of your head (awareness of this area is of special importance to people who experience sinus and tension headaches).

If your timer goes off before you finish, you can decide whether to continue scanning for a few more minutes, or pick it up during a later sitting. If you finish the scan and your timer still hasn't gone off, spend the rest of your time focusing on your breathing.

Journal Exercise 3-2: The Body Scan

In this journal entry, describe your initial experience with the body scan exercise. Answer the questions below to help you articulate your thoughts and feelings:

- Where do you notice you are carrying the most physical tension in your body?

- Does that area of tension correlate at all with any physical problems you experience, like headaches, backaches, or stomachaches?

- What parts of the exercise were most successful for you?

- What was your greatest challenge in completing this exercise?

- How difficult was it to pay attention to and control your breathing?

- How difficult was it to control your attention during the scan?

- After you completed the body scan exercise, how did you feel?

Over the next few weeks you will want to practice the body scan at least every day until you can complete an entire, thorough scan in just five or ten minutes. After each scan it is a good idea to note the date and time in your journal and take a minute to record what you are learning and experiencing in each practice session.

THE RELAXATION RESPONSE

The relaxation response was discovered in the early 1970s by Herbert Benson (1975), a cardiologist at Harvard Medical School. In the United States the relaxation response is considered the foremost tool in mind-body medicine, one that physicians and psychologists have been teaching to their patients for more than thirty years. It has been demonstrated to be effective in the treatment of virtually every disease, disorder, and syndrome that a modern human being can get. It is the frontline treatment for hypertension, cardiovascular disease, high blood pressure, insomnia, chronic pain, and substance abuse. The relaxation response has been used as the control-group treatment in thousands of medical studies, and it has been found to be just as effective as far more invasive and expensive alternatives.

You may notice a number of similarities between the body scan exercise, described earlier, and the relaxation response. But the relaxation response requires you to be more active both physically and mentally. The goal of the body scan is simple awareness; the goal of the relaxation response is, well, relaxation. You practice the body scan as a form of meditation that increases your awareness of your physical being. You practice the relaxation response to put yourself in a physically and mentally relaxed state. With practice the relaxation response will become a reflex, sort of like smiling or laughing. You will use relaxation to get you out of "hot" situations—a deliberate action you can take to get your physical being under control.

Practice the relaxation response twice a day, for ten to fifteen minutes at a time. It is best to do this in a quiet, calm place. Sitting on a chair or mat is recommended, because if you practice the relaxation response while lying down you might fall asleep before you complete it. (Of course, you can turn this to your advantage at bedtime, by practicing the relaxation response when it is time to go to sleep.) If you are concerned about time, set a kitchen timer for ten or fifteen minutes before you begin each session, and turn the timer face away from you so you're not distracted by how much time is left.

1. Choose a sound, an image, a prayer, a mantra, a color, or even a wonderful smell that means something to you, something that you associate with being calm and serene, something that has positive emotional connections for you. Make sure this is an image or sound you can muster up at will. I like to pick visual themes, like a beautiful old birch tree on the corner of my property, or the image of a lake at sunset, but you should pick whatever seems right for you.

2. Repeat this sound or focus on this image until it is an automatic thought or experience that you can bring to mind simply by flipping a switch in your brain.

3. Close your eyes (after you finish reading the rest of the steps, of course!).

4. As in the body scan, but a bit less methodically, pay attention to all the muscle groups in your body, beginning with the feet and progressing in jumps from feet to calves, thighs, abdomen, shoulders, neck, and head. As you focus on each muscle group, tighten the muscles in that group as hard as you can, and hold the tension as long as you can before it becomes uncomfortable.

5. After you tighten each muscle group, let it go all at once, and experience the extraordinary feeling that results. This feeling is the essence of the relaxation response. Continue this tighten-and-release sequence for each muscle group.

6. Simply breathe slowly and naturally and, when you are fully relaxed, bring your personal relaxation image or stimulus to your conscious attention. You are now pairing the wonderful feeling of your resting muscles with a pleasant mental event.

7. Every time you exhale, deepen the feeling of relaxation a little further. If necessary, tighten a pesky muscle group during the inhalation, but then let it completely relax on the exhale.

8. Keep your attention tuned to both your personal relaxation image or stimulus and the sensations in your body. If your mind begins to wander, bring it back by focusing more carefully and deeply on the image or stimulus you have selected.

9.   When the time is up, just sit there and notice how good you feel. When you're ready, open your eyes and take in the world around you.

Journal Exercise 3-3: The Relaxation Response

As you've probably guessed, I want you to practice this exercise and then record your experience in your journal. Answer the questions below to help you identify and articulate your thoughts and feelings:

- Did you notice which muscle groups were carrying the most tension?

- Does the tension in these muscle groups correspond to any physical and medical problems you have been experiencing?

- If you felt any pain before you began the exercise, had that pain lessened or even disappeared by the time you finished the exercise?

- Did your personal relaxation image change in intensity or vividness during the course of the exercise?

- How would you describe the feeling you had when the exercise was complete?

The fun thing about this exercise is that you can teach your kids, your spouse, your gym partner, and even your parents how to do this, too. You can become an instant relaxation guru, and nobody will think you are especially weird or strange for doing it.

If you have a blood-pressure or heart-rate monitor, you might find it interesting to take a reading before and after your practice; I think you will be very impressed by the result. According to lots of published studies, your blood pressure should drop by five to ten points (on both the systolic and the diastolic scales) after you have acquired the relaxation response. You need to understand, however, that these effects will only be maintained for as long as you keep practicing the relaxation response on a regular basis.

At some point you will probably decide that you enjoy doing either the body scan or the relaxation response more than the other. But whichever you prefer, make sure you practice it regularly, because your goal is to be able to relax on command, when you are confronted with a stressor. We are ultimately going to replace your old self-abusive way of dealing with the world with a new, serene way that will help you live to a ripe old age.

Beyond the Body: The Importance of Human Interaction

Getting back to evolution and your stress response, it seems highly unlikely that the early hominids sat in their caves and did body scans. They probably didn't encourage the frustrated members of their hunting party to visualize a wildebeest roasting over a fire while deeply relaxing their calf muscles. It could have happened, but there is no archeological evidence on the point.

What does seem pretty obvious is that human beings are still primates, and we know that all primates control their stress by hanging out with other primates. Early in this chapter I mentioned that anger effectively blocks the most important natural system that human beings rely on to recover from prolonged or excessive periods of hyperarousal. That natural way to recover is to make contact with your fellow human beings—to make a sincere effort to extend yourself beyond your own private experience. And, of course, anger makes it extraordinarily difficult to do that.

CARING FOR YOURSELF BY TAKING CARE OF OTHERS

Here's some good news for you. Even if your anger has left you absolutely friendless and without any family, you can get some relief just by going out and buying a plant. No kidding! Elderly folks in nursing homes actually live longer and have fewer illnesses if they are given plants to take care of. If the nursing home staff takes care of the plant for them, the patient shows no improvement. It is the physical and mental investment that a person makes in the plant that helps keep them healthy and alive.

So start with a ficus, and, if you're successful, you could work all the way up to taking care of a dog or a cat or a gerbil. In fact, I bet that a lot of angry people take better care of their pets than they do themselves or their friends. Pets don't talk back, and they are generally happy to see you when you come home from work. But don't you think you might be capable of caring for something a little more significant than a geranium and some tropical fish?

Be a Healthy Primate

As the famous Stanford University biologist Robert Sapolsky noted in his fascinating book *Why Zebras Don't Get Ulcers* (1998), numerous studies document that healthy, well-adjusted, and reproductively successful primates in the wild possess robust immune systems, low cholesterol, and nicely regulated blood pressure—and they have fun and enjoy life, too. Most of them, in fact, do not have house plants or raise cocker spaniels (although primates in captivity do seem to be fascinated by kittens).

What these critters do to relieve their stress and keep their minds healthy is to act like grandpas, dads, brothers, uncles, friends, teammates, and buddies. They spend lots of time, in fact, playing with kids, hugging other primates, engaging in mutual (nonsexual) grooming, hanging about, tickling, giving back rubs, playing tag, telling tall stories, playing poker, making love, and in general relishing every day that they are given. They enjoy a relaxed and secure old age in the company of their near and extended kin, and as they age they become the fonts of wisdom about how to find the good blueberry bushes and what to do about the young troublemakers in the group.

By contrast, the angry, aggressive, restless, and combative primates clearly enjoy the short-term benefits of being dominant (access to better food, better nests, and more frequent sex). But they are never dominant for long (there's always somebody younger, stronger, and more clever watching for them to reveal a moment of weakness). And when they are removed from power they discover that there is no room for them in the group they once dominated. Their old age is spent either alone or among strangers. Their coworkers may attend their funerals—but mostly just to make sure that they really are dead.

A CONCLUDING MEDITATION: BEING HUMAN

Journal Exercise 3-4: Be a Human Being

The following mindful meditation is probably the most important one in the book. Find yourself a quiet and pleasant place to sit. Do a quick body scan; breathe away some tension, and locate the center of your consciousness. Now, spend about twenty minutes reflecting on how you can find a friend to hang out with, a partner to give a back rub to, an elderly person who needs someone to reminisce with, a boy who wants to be coached and challenged, a teenager who can be taught some amazing skill, a grandchild you can tickle, or, if all else fails, a geranium that needs some water.

Use your journal to record what you discover during this meditation, and then go out and try to live the lesson as if your life depended on it, because, you know, it really does.

4

Heart and Soul: Connecting with Other Human Beings

The heart and soul of mindfulness is the realization that every human being on the planet is interconnected with and interdependent on every other human being and living thing on the planet. The terrorist in a war-torn country, the little old lady down the street, the politicians in Washington—they are all connected with each of us every day of our lives. This is an idea that few of us are fully aware of or are really prepared to deal with. Angry men have even more difficulty accepting this interconnectedness than the rest of us do. They are almost totally preoccupied with themselves, and they seem to perceive that their lives stand alone and apart from the lives of others. As a result, their anger is frequently triggered by people who have deliberately or accidentally intruded into their comfort zone. But, on the other hand, if I came by their house with a check for $10,000 and in so doing parked on their grass, left their front door open, and also happened to be of the wrong race, nationality, or sexual orientation, would they really feel deprived if they didn't get to tell me off?

Well, of course not. And that is precisely the point I am trying to convey. According to Buddhist philosophy, we are interconnected all the time—not just when there is someone at the door giving away money, but all the time, even when we are lonely, scared, irritable, and confused.

JUSTIFIED ANGER

From a mindfulness perspective, as Jon Kabat-Zinn (1994) has remarked, "anger is the price that we pay for being attached to a narrow view of being right [while] the collective pain we cause others and ourselves bleeds our souls." In my work counseling men I am consistently struck by how much anger is directly connected with absolutist views about what is right and wrong—views that are justified by an extensive catalog of abstract principles about proper human conduct, a great deal of which are defined by rigid sex-specific cultural norms. The vast majority of angry young men I work with see themselves not only as the last bastion of what is right and proper and acceptable but also as the target of myriad moral infractions that they encounter on a daily basis.

Scratch the surface of any young man's anger, in my experience, and you will find the wildly beating heart of an enraged, defiant victim. This is the root of what Sandra Thomas (2003) has termed *justified anger*. Indeed, a group of anger researchers found that perceptions of victimization are frequently the primary reason for overt anger manifested by people in their workplaces (Aquino, Douglas, and Martinko 2004). People don't just walk around being angry, they walk around being angry at specific people and situations. Anger is thus not only deeply personal but also profoundly interpersonal.

The most obvious place where we come face to face with the interpersonal nature of anger is when we decide that some other person has intentionally violated our decrees about what is right, moral, and just. If somebody screws up they had better be made to understand that they deserve one big world of hurt, particularly if it looks like they screwed up on purpose. And the angry guys line up around the block to volunteer for the job of delivering the righteous punishment that the guilty deserve. Researchers estimate that 94 percent of the time anger is directed at other people, with the bulk of it pointed toward family members, friends, and coworkers (Del Vecchio and O'Leary 2004). You almost want to feel sorry for angry guys who have to live in a world populated by so many imperfect relatives, friends, and coworkers.

According to Marvin Levine (2000), the most likely reasons for us to be justifiably angry at other people include the following:

- Someone causes you physical pain (accidental or not).

- You are frustrated by someone's incompetence or intransigence.

- Some inferior man (or woman or child) disrespects you, especially in public.

- Someone treats you unfairly.

Justified Anger and the Breakdown of Compassion

From a Buddhist perspective, all anger, but especially justified anger, is seen as a manifestation of the breakdown of compassion, reflecting not just a failure of sufficient emotional self-control but also a fundamental loss of what it means to be a connected, aware, and interdependent being. Intense social and emotional isolation is the ultimate price of an angry person's distress. And this lack of human interconnection is about as close as you can come to a complete loss of what it means to be a human being. In fact, this loss is so devastating that Buddhist teaching recognizes anger as one of the three greatest destructive forces, along with greed and delusion, that human beings can experience.

Moreover, since anger is itself rooted in human greed and nurtured by ignorance and delusion, this emotion is the epitome of human suffering. This emotional affliction is rooted in an alienating preoccupation with selfish desire, which derives from an unenlightened understanding of the self and the world. It is for this reason that the problem of anger is located at the center of Buddhist concern for human well-being.

Columbia University Buddhism scholar Robert Thurman (Thurman and Wise 1999) summarized the Buddhist perspective on the connection between anger and suffering as follows:

One of the great sources of our suffering is hatred, and all of its variation: resentment, anger, bitterness, dislike, irritation, aggressiveness, hostility. Hate is very powerful. When we are gripped by hatred we go into a rage and become completely out of control. We smash up our own beloved body and commit suicide. We smash up people whom we love, wives, husbands, children, parents. Rage can turn us into a complete maniac or demon—temporarily. It's one of the most dangerous kinds of energies, very difficult to control. Any force we can marshal within ourselves to prevent and forestall the explosive moment of rage is really beneficial. (6)

Anger and Human Isolation

As I mentioned above, anger is rooted in the preoccupation with the self, and the impossible desires that come with an unenlightened understanding of the self and the world. The challenge for the angry man who wishes to reduce his suffering is to wake up from the dream that his desires can be satisfied, his obstacles eradicated, and his suffering eliminated through the application of righteous force. He must recognize that he can relieve his unrelenting suffering only by finding some way to regain connection with his true nature as a human being. As the Buddha taught, the most effective way to reduce anger is to make a concentrated study within oneself of the thoughts, feelings, and actions that make anger come and those that make it go away (Levine 2000).

Anger and Revenge

Anger can often be seen as the product of what Shakespeare might have called "a mind diseased," a fundamental impairment in the way a person comprehends and responds to the world around him. In addition, as the ancient Greek philosopher Aristotle (1960, 93) observed, "anger is always attended by a certain pleasure arising from the expectation of revenge." Indeed, The Iliad, Homer's epic poem about the anger of both gods and men, reminds us that much anger is about coercing compliance from those who have made the serious error of disagreeing with us. One of the Noble Truths the Buddha taught was that our suffering is directly tied to our constant and sometimes quite intense desires. We pursue these desires in ways that often harm and degrade others, especially when that desire is either for revenge or driven by greed.

It can be easy to see how the pursuit of our desires ends up punishing others, if we are willing to open our eyes to these effects. The effects on our own well-being, however, are often more subtle but can certainly be equally corrosive and destructive. It's not that the angry person's desires are fundamentally different than my own or anyone else's; it's that in living so intensely with his desires he has lost any real awareness of the suffering his pursuit of those desires has caused—both in himself and in the people he loves.

Confronting Your Own Righteousness

Understandably, it is both easy and common for angry people to become quite attached to their anger and to actively resist identifying their chronic anger as a source of problems in their lives. The founder of rational emotive behavior therapy, Albert Ellis, would energetically say that all this angry suffering is the price we pay for spending much of our waking lives thinking, talking, and interacting with others as if we were Moses. We hike through the wilderness, climb the mountain, receive the word of God from a burning bush, and descend the mountain to declare The Law. Deviations from the law we have laid down enrage us; we are compelled to punish the lawbreakers with righteous indignation, completely unaware of our self-indulgence as we take the position of God's stand-in here on earth (Ellis and Harper 1997).

PUTTING THE FEAR OF GOD IN YOUR KIDS

A while ago, a news story ran on television about a man who had started a company that specialized in selling wooden paddles and other objects that parents could use for punishing their kids. The paddles are decorated with various Old Testament verses that encourage the physical punishment of unruly children, and the phrase "Use with Love" is burned at the tip of each paddle. Business was good. Lots of people wanted to be able to free their conscience about beating their kids, and this entrepreneur had found a profitable way for them to be able to do so—with encouragement from God. Knocking your kids around is, presumably, a special prerogative of very righteous parents who are willing to invest a few bucks in religious paraphernalia.

Consider, however, that every single day in the United States of America three children die as a result of child abuse in the home. Most (84.5 percent) of these children are younger than six years old, and 41 percent are under the age of one. In fact, in the most recent report available, the United States Department of Health and Human Services (2005) reports that infant homicide reached a thirty-year high in 2003, and that 3 million suspected cases of child abuse are reported to authorities every year. The children's parents represented 81 percent of the offenders. Approximately half of these adults were drunk or stoned at the time of their crime; the other half, evidently, were sober. The drunk and stoned parents probably belong in jail and/or rehab, but what about the 1.5 million parents (and these are just the ones who are being investigated by the authorities) who abuse their kids with a clear and fully functioning mind?

No reasonably well-informed person can doubt that the vast majority of these abused and murdered children were victimized by angry adults. It is hard to know what is really going on in the minds of the drunk and the stoned, but we can be pretty certain that at least half of the victims were brutalized by a sober person who had found some way to justify their barbaric acts.

As Robert Thurman (2005, 44) points out, "there are those who consider anger something magnificent, as imparting 'greatness of mind,'" whose anger creates in them a state of "morbid enlargement" that other mortals lack. But Thurman goes on to quote the Roman philosopher, Seneca, who wrote,

> There is nothing about anger, not even in the apparent extravagance of its disdain for gods and men, that is great or noble. If anyone does think that anger makes a great mind manifest, he might think the same about self-indulgence—with its wish to be borne on ivory, dressed in purple, [and] roofed with gold . . . (45)

Angry Legacies

Angry parents create enraged, defiant, angry kids. Abusive parents create bullies, and they set the example that will repeat the pattern of anger, abuse, and violence far into the future. The fact that parents justify abusing their kids in the name of righteousness must be one of the greatest travesties in all of human history. That there are people out there who have found a way to make money off it makes me nearly speechless.

But the real issue is how to stop it. Robert Thurman proposes a solution that is so radically rational that it almost defies credibility. To solve this problem, he says, four things are required: *courage, justice, endurance,* and *wisdom.* And, if I might be permitted to append to his list, I would add *love* and *compassion.*

I hope you are beginning to see that the legacy of anger, especially anger that is directed toward the people you love, must be defeated by an overwhelming commitment to uphold rational, humane values. These are all, of course, values that are nourished, cherished, and liberated by the practice of mindfulness.

Journal Exercise 4-1: Your Anger Legacy

This mindfulness exercise asks you to examine and accept the legacy of anger that was handed down to you by your parents. In your journal, describe what it was like to be the target of your parents' anger. If your mother or father hit you, slapped you, or took a belt to you, how did it make you feel? Did you ever promise yourself that you would get revenge? Did you ever think about how you would treat your own kids someday? Was there a difference between their rational punishments for breaking rules and the like, and their unjust punishments that they inflicted when they were angry?

What role did righteousness play in your parents' anger? Do you think, in retrospect, that they felt that their anger was justified by their authority over you? What do you think about this today?

Now, here are the really hard questions: In what ways have you brought this pattern of angry righteousness into the lives of your own children? Do you want to see them perpetuate this family tradition? What can you do to prevent it from being passed along to your grandchildren?

Do you have the courage, endurance, wisdom, love, and compassion to make it so?

UNREALISTIC ANGER: THE ANGRY IMPULSE AND THE INNOCENT BYSTANDER

Closely related to the idea of justified anger is the concept of *unrealistic anger*, defined as the negative emotion experienced when "trying to assert control over something that does not need correcting or that cannot be corrected" (Sapolsky 1998, 334). Unrealistic anger thrusts all of us, especially young men, into a self-perpetuating series of emotional battles that, as we saw in the last chapter, are biologically dangerous and even lethal. Anger, with its corrosive power, is fed by an emotional core of craving, aversion, and ignorance, which are the central focus of a Buddhist approach to understanding human suffering.

Angry Men and the Burden of Always Being Right

Both justified and unrealistic anger are deeply imprinted on young men as masculine virtues by a culture that glorifies strength and violence and at the same time is deeply distrustful of authority and convention. The recent Hollywood film *Fight Club* showcases the pervasiveness of this highly resilient strand of American masculinity training. The bald fact is that many men in our culture feel compelled to invest large amounts of time and energy in demanding respect and saving face, as well as defending against any appearance of weakness, incompetence, or uncertainty.

Because we men are expected to "perform" our masculinity both in public and in private around the clock, any challenge to our competence or authority, and any sign of disrespect—whether on the street, at work, or in our homes—is seen as a significant threat to our credibility as worthy human beings. Psychologists and psychobiologists might call the anger that results from one of these threats "unrealistic" and profoundly unhealthy—but that's not the way it looks to the angry man, and it certainly isn't the way it feels to him.

The regular practice of mindfulness offers men a psychological buffer zone, a place for introspection, and a retreat from the angry rhetoric of unrealistic anger. I have found that practicing mindfulness can and often does provide a very real sanctuary for men, particularly young men, where they can take stock of themselves and their relationship to the world. Perhaps most important, they can take stock of their relationship with a whole variety of authoritarian teachings, and begin the process of sorting out and owning what is true, important, and real. By adopting a mindful orientation toward their personal experience they will almost certainly experience a wide range of emotional, psychological, interpersonal, and spiritual benefits.

MY ANGRY SAGA

The other day I needed to use my lunch hour to go to the supermarket to buy a bag of dog food for my ancient labrador retriever, Sophie, and some Halloween treats for the neighborhood kids. Between this and that and the traffic, I got to the store with barely enough time to do my shopping and order a sandwich at a fast food drive-through.

When I was ready to pay for my groceries, all of the checkouts had long lines, but one of the automatic scanner machines was free. So I dropped the forty-pound bag of kibble on the scale, expecting to be out of the store in five minutes. However, for some stupid reason you can't drop forty pounds of dog food on the scale—it's not designed to hold that much weight, and it broke. And the clerk in charge didn't know how to fix it. Actually, he thought he knew how to fix it, but after ten tries the scanner was still unconscious. The clerk appeared perfectly willing to spend the rest of his shift trying to make everything right, but I didn't have that kind of time. My blood began to boil, and the bag of treats began to melt in my clenched fist. Within thirty seconds I felt my anger rising. I was angry at the corporation that owned the grocery store. I was angry at the automatic checkout scanner. I was angry at the clerk. I was furious at the dog food that I had by now picked up and put down eleven times. I was angry at the neighborhood kids, who would think badly of me if I didn't provide them with a nearly lethal sugar overload once a year. I was outraged that not only was I a complete idiot but I was also going to miss my lunch!

Then it got even worse. I realized that if my wife had picked up the dog food and the treats during the weekend, none of this would have happened. Then I started getting mad at the dog, who was, of course, sound asleep at home and dreaming about her next meal. I started having homicidal thoughts about the trick-or-treaters. The thought actually crossed my mind that I would buy only the dog food and just tell the little ninjas and princesses that they could go to hell—I am just too busy to screw around with all this Halloween crap. If you want treats, get a job and buy your own.

I was astonished to observe how easily and how quickly my dukkha-creating machinery kicked in and began spreading a dark cloud of unhappiness all around me. But then, after a few seconds of emotional turmoil, my rational self began to kick in. I realized that my thinking was getting all messed up by my selfish emotions (My precious time is so important!), and that what I really needed to do was to start thinking like a good human being, instead of acting like a jerk. I realized that, hey, this is the store I shop in all the time. I know this clerk and he knows me. I also realized that dealing with customers who have tantrums because they aren't smart enough to use the technology can't be a fun way to spend forty hours a week, even if only a small percentage of your customers act like idiots. Moreover, I love my dog like crazy, and on her list of daily joys mealtime is only second to the absolute thrill she gets when I come home from work. Not only that, but Halloween is my favorite holiday of the entire year—a day set aside just for little kids and their parents. I realized, at that moment, that I needed to sober up my monkey mind! I needed to follow rule 4 from chapter 1 (I Am Not My Anger!). I have anger, and I can even provoke and watch it. But I am not my anger. Fortunately, I was able to use my practice of mindfulness to stop myself from creating more suffering in the lives of the people around me, including the store clerk, the trick-or-treaters, my wife, and my dog. I broke the scanner, yes, but I hope I did not add much more suffering to the universe than that.

Paying Attention to Connections

What was both fascinating and troubling about my angry episode was how interconnected it was. It was possible, I suppose, for me to have held myself entirely and exclusively to blame for the whole sorry affair, but that's not what I did. Within the space of mere seconds I managed to implicate a store employee, a corporation, a labrador retriever, the neighborhood kids, and even my spouse in my emotional thunderstorm. Why did I need to find so many other people to blame for an accident that could have happened to anyone trying to scan something a bit too heavy? Why was it so important to see my troubles as someone else's fault? Is my self-esteem so low, and are my problem-solving skills so deficient, that I can't take responsibility for my own actions?

The answer, I think, is a bit of a Buddhist paradox. I am driven to infect everyone around me with my anger precisely because I am so utterly and completely interdependent with everyone around me. My anger, my frustration, my embarrassment, and even my breaking the machine *only* occur because I live in a world extensively populated by other people. Anger, in some sense, is proof that I am not alone, proof that I am a human being, proof that I rather desperately need other people to pay attention to me. The good news is that my anger is positive proof that I am still alive. The bad news is that everything I do when I am angry has the effect of driving people away from me—at precisely those moments when I need human contact the most.

The Frenchman and the Devil

The dilemma angry people confront is how to break through the miasma of their emotional upset to make contact with their true human natures. Anger becomes a sort of alien force that not only locks them away from their own Buddha natures but also keeps them from making fundamental connections with their family, friends, and other people who care about them.

This phenomenon reminds me of a remarkable episode in the life of the French psychiatrist Pierre Janet, who basically invented modern psychiatry in the early 1900s. Janet was attempting to treat a frenzied young man who was locked in a state of insanity. The man was so intent upon killing himself that Janet had been forced to have him tightly restrained while he struggled to break through to his patient's unconscious mind.

Janet knew, in accordance with the standard medical practices of the day, that the only way the man, Achilles, could be cured was to surrender to a deep hypnosis, where the secret cause of his madness could be identified and addressed. But all of Janet's attempts at hypnosis were thwarted by an evil spirit that appeared to have possessed Achilles and invaded his soul. Every time Janet tried to hypnotize his patient, this devil within Achilles' mind roared with laughter, and Achilles' madness intensified even further.

But then Janet had a brilliant idea. He challenged the devil to demonstrate his power over Achilles' body and soul. Janet challenged the devil to raise Achilles' arms; and the devil did so at once. Janet next challenged the devil to make Achilles' eyes open, and open they did. This went on for a while, with Janet ultimately provoking the devil to conduct a thorough body scan and relaxation response on poor Achilles, at which point Janet turned to the devil and whispered (in French, of course), "Well, if you really are that powerful, then let me see you hypnotize him!"

Achilles at once went into a deep hypnotic trance, and, *voila!* Janet was able to use his powerful hypnotic therapy to get the information he needed (it turned out that Achilles had been unfaithful to his new wife while away from home on business) to restore his patient to complete mental health.

What I am suggesting is that anger is our modern-day equivalent of Achilles' devil. It mocks us, it roars at us, and it defies us. And yet we still have the power within us to liberate ourselves from the madness our anger poisons us with—and once we have exorcised that demon we can mindfully enter into connection with other people in ways that will transform our current unhappiness into the ability to live and work and love as complete human beings.

I am also suggesting, moreover, that mindfulness can do the job that hypnosis did for Janet's unfortunate patient. That job is the recovery and restoration of a complete, socially aware, and responsible human being—through the power of the human mind.

MINDFULNESS AND HUMAN CONNECTION

From a Buddhist perspective, the distress that angry people experience and create is seen as the product of the social isolation and the emotional alienation that comes from the mistaken belief in the illusion of separateness. This problem is particularly severe in North American men, the undisputed archbishops of the church of extreme individualism.

The distress of the angry man is not rooted in the rush to buy dog food and Halloween treats, or even the prospect of missing lunch. The problem is not that the world is full of idiots, or that too many or too few people are acting like perfectionists. The problem isn't even that you are hardwired to be an impulsive "hot responder" in emotion-provoking situations. The problem really isn't in your biology, your sociology, or even your disturbed way of looking at the world around you.

The problem is in your character.

The Impossible Desires of the Uninformed Heart

The devil that has captured your soul and your imagination is fundamental human *ignorance*. It is ignorance of the true human condition that both stems from and perpetuates an impossible preoccupation with the self, selfish desires, and the illusion that you are special, separate, and uniquely challenged.

Anger is rooted in an unenlightened understanding of both the self and the world. The cure is essentially a moral revolution within the most profound center of the person, a revolution that cannot be achieved until a man awakens from the dream, or illusion, that his desires can be finally and fully satisfied, all his obstacles eradicated, and all his suffering completely eliminated. This illusion must be replaced by an awakening—some would call it an *enlightenment*—that comes from the realization of compassionate regard for the self and everyone else in the world.

The Tale of the Woman Whose Grief Was Unbearable

The tale of the woman whose grief was unbearable is one of the most important teaching stories in all of Buddhist lore. A woman once confronted the Buddha and accused him of not understanding the pain and suffering of ordinary people. She asserted that she could never accept the *dharma* (teachings) of the Buddha because her life was full of rage and sorrow since her young child had died of a disease. The Buddha had taught that right-minded people could put an end to their suffering by transforming their minds and their lives, but this woman knew that her sorrow was so deep that it could never be assuaged.

The Buddha listened carefully to her story and communicated that he understood the depth of her pain and the pervasiveness of her anger. He then made her an offer. If she would go door to door throughout the town and collect one grain of rice from each family who had not known the sharp pain of loss, he would then cook those grains of rice for her in a special pot. Once she had eaten that rice, he promised, she would never experience suffering again.

So the woman went to every home in the town, and inquired whether the people who lived inside had escaped human suffering. Day after day and night after night she continued, desperate in her search for the rice that would guarantee her freedom from her pain. But, of course, every family she visited had a story to tell of their own pain and loss. After she had visited every last house, she returned to the place where the Buddha was staying and admitted that she was returning to him empty-handed. And that, of course, was when she became enlightened.

Journal Exercise 4-2: Going Door to Door

You undoubtedly know any number of people who have experienced significant losses in the recent past. Their loss might have been caused by divorce, a job loss, a serious illness, a death in the family, or the discovery that a trusted friend had betrayed them. Your task is to put yourself in the position of the woman in the story and make yourself available to them to hear their account of what happened to them.

Interview one or two people who have recently experienced a significant loss in their life. Your job is just to listen, not to offer any advice, and try to be as aware as you can of the pain and distress this person felt.

Record a summary of these stories in your journal, paying attention not just to the events that transpired but also to what it meant to this person and his or her family. Then write about your human response to the experience of listening to this fellow human being. Really focus on the emotions you experienced, and what you did when you experienced those emotions. Finally, describe what you communicated or hoped to communicate to this person, and reflect on what impact your listening might have had on their suffering and unhappiness.

Note: When you invite someone to tell you about his or her experience, try as hard as you can to use the following three active-listening techniques:

- Don't try to change the subject or fix anything.

- Don't offer any advice or utter any bullshit.

■   Just be there, as fearlessly as you can.

Conclude your exercise by mindfully observing your experience trying to use to these three active-listening techniques during your conversation. Write about your observations.

COMPASSION, ANGER, AND PAIN

The Buddha's motive in sending the woman to every home in town, just like my motive in asking you to complete the exercise above, was more complicated than just a desire to get an angry person off his back. It wasn't to make her feel ashamed of her selfishness (although you may have noticed that emotion as you wrote your journal entry), or even to make her forget her own troubles for a little while. His motive was to structure her experience in such a way that her Buddha nature would be *awakened.*

Human beings rarely achieve enlightenment simply by enduring their own suffering. Enlightenment is achieved when a person experiences genuine connection with other people. But if that is all there is to it, why didn't the Buddha just advise the woman to go to a baseball game with a bunch of her friends?

The answer is that the sort of genuine connection and interdependency at the heart of enlightenment is rooted in the experience of *compassion.* Unless all this woman's friends were die-hard Chicago Cubs fans, a baseball game would probably not lead to the sort of compassionate connection that engenders enlightened awareness of the nature of the world.

I have an interesting theory about all this that I hope you will find some truth in. My hunch, based on working with hundreds of angry men over the years, is that the connection between compassion, anger, and pain is a whole lot more than coincidental. My theory, in fact, is that, if anything, angry men are actually *more* compassionate than most human beings. It is their compassionate nature that makes them aware of and sensitive to everything that is wrong in the world. I think that people who rarely or never get angry are not Buddhas in disguise. Rather, they are probably somewhat unobservant and/or indifferent, whereas angry men are highly vigilant and typically over-invested in the world around them. I'm suggesting, in effect, that angry men may be a lot closer to enlightenment than the cold-blooded guys who are simply not affected by all the suffering that exists in this world.

I can support my case by pointing to the data on career burnout. The people who burn out are never the mindless commuters who show up every day mainly so they can collect their paychecks at the end of the week. The people who burn out are virtually always the people who care deeply and passionately about what they are doing for a living but for whatever reason lack the power to make significant changes in the system.

And what characterizes those who experience burnout? These are people who suffer from chronic immune system deficiencies, people who experience episodes of depression, and people who are (you know what I am going to say next) *angry* at the indifference and stupidity of "the system."

Back to Compassion (and Mindfulness)

So we all need to take a lesson from the late Dr. Janet. We need to figure out how to trick the devil, not torture ourselves in a fruitless and pointless struggle to overpower him. We need to figure out some way to retain our ability to see the world as it really is, and yet use the power of our humanity to accomplish what needs to be done. The power to accomplish this difficult but entirely possible trick is in the experience of compassion, which is rooted in our connections with our fellow human beings. And the way we stay aware of these connections, and stay connected to the power that we derive from them, is through the active, regular process of *mindfulness*.

As I've said before, the whole point of mindfulness is to learn to pay attention, on purpose, in the present moment, without judgment, for the sake of greater awareness, clarity, and overall well-being. But pay attention to what?

Well, I think the deep answer is that it doesn't really matter what we pay attention to, because all mindfulness leads in the same direction. When a person commits himself to paying attention in an open way, without falling prey to his own likes and dislikes, opinions and prejudices, projections and expectations, he truly opens himself up to the present moment, and when he does so he will become amazingly aware of the possibilities that exist in the world around him. And all of those possibilities are deeply and even profoundly connected to the lives of other people. Thus is born the discovery of the deep interconnection between all human beings, and, indeed, all living things. And that interconnection is the wellspring of human compassion.

Journal Exercise 4-3: Practicing Mindfulness and Compassion

Before you start, set a kitchen timer for thirty minutes to one hour. Begin by either sitting in a straight-backed chair with your feet firmly on the ground, lying on a mat, or sitting on a cushion. Spend at least ten minutes focusing on your breathing; breathe through your nose deeply from your belly in a series of slow, deep, intentional breaths. Focus your attention, either by counting your breaths in groups of ten, or by counting the seconds during each inhale and exhale.

After your breath is stable and regular, shift your attention to the present moment; attend to each second of each minute, trying to keep your mind free of distractions by attending to your breath with serious interest. Soon you will notice how unawareness will challenge your well-being. All kinds of old, insignificant thoughts and memories will float up to the surface; just breathe them away. Many other distractions will compete for your attention; again, just breathe them away.

When you are ready, focus your mind's eye on the face of the person you love most in this world. Keep your attention on this image, and let it completely fill your consciousness. Pay attention to details that you haven't noticed for a long time—perhaps not until this very moment. Open yourself up to everything this person means to you, and free yourself to experience the love that you feel for this person. Continue your breathing as you keep this person's presence fully centered in your mind.

When your time is up, open your journal and record your feelings. Reflect on how you might most truthfully and directly communicate the compassion you experience when you are connected with this person. How can you best share this experience with the person who has just been in your mind's eye?

FINDING AND GIVING SUPPORT

The final section of this chapter is almost entirely therapeutic. It contains a message of hope, reconciliation, and perhaps even redemption.

First you need to answer this question: do you understand and accept that there is a causal link between selfishness, self-centeredness, self-righteousness, emotional isolation, and the experience of anger? If you do, read on. If you don't, go out and collect your own data. Observe angry people, observe yourself when you are angry. With the exception of the emotions felt by those who are caught up in a life-or-death battle to protect their loved ones from a squad of unrestrained psychopathic predators, the anger we witness and experience is clearly rooted in profound ignorance about what really matters in this life (Novaco 1996).

On Making Human Contact

Angry men routinely commit two major sins against human nature. First, they try to minimize and avoid human contact and, second, they find it almost impossible to both seek out and gracefully accept support from the people who care about them. This is a pattern that is sometimes cute in two-year-olds (as in "I wanna do it myself!"), but it is ruinous in people who consider themselves adults.

One of the odd things that you may observe is that you actually feel pretty good about yourself and the world when you are in a situation where you have the opportunity to lend assistance to another person. Whether you are teaching someone how to do something new and difficult, or having someone you like and respect come to you for advice about a problem he or she is having, it feels really good to make someone else's life a little better or a little easier.

Perhaps I am a little biased on this point because I have devoted my life to the twin "helping professions" of counseling and teaching, but I see evidence of the joy that men experience from helping others all around me every day. When I recently asked a group of twenty college men to write down the very best experiences they have had in college, every single one wrote down something that had to do with helping someone else out, whether as a tutor or a coach or just a fully present friend. *All* the guys found that their lives were significantly enriched when they contributed in some way to someone else's life.

When I turned the question around and asked them to think of a time when they had felt good because they had received a kindness from someone, the answers came more slowly and required a lot more thought. Guys told me it usually felt good when they received help from a parent, a long-term friend, or a coach or teacher, though they were a little nervous about receiving help with something important from a girlfriend, a younger student, or a stranger. The experiences of receiving help that they recalled most fondly, however, were from an older brother. It felt especially good to feel connected to a role model whom they looked up to, especially one who knew all their faults and weaknesses.

The following exercise takes advantage of the fact that it is easier for most guys to do nice than to receive nice. Who knows—if you can pull this off successfully, maybe you'll even find the courage to accept a little bit of help the next time you need it.

Journal Exercise 4-4: Random, Anonymous Acts of Kindness

The purpose of this activity couldn't be simpler. Your task is to walk around in the world looking for opportunities to commit small, seemingly random, anonymous acts of kindness. Then record in your journal the details of your act, and carefully monitor *how* you felt after each event.

The real challenge in this assignment is to keep it truly anonymous. You are probably going to be tempted to take credit for your actions, and let the lucky recipient of your kindness know exactly to whom he or she is now in debt. But you must resist this temptation. The Buddha inside you requires you to be stealthy, observant, and completely anonymous.

For a real treat, let your kids in on your secret mission, and encourage them to find ways that they too can commit random, anonymous acts of kindness in their own lives. Have some fun sharing your stories with each other.

I need to warn you about one aspect of the above exercise that might shake you a little: people's responses to being the targets of random, anonymous acts of kindness can be quite varied. Some people may act as if they are entirely accustomed to anonymous folks doing nice things for them, and others may barely notice. Worse, some may become suspicious and imagine that a dangerous plot may be at work against them. Recently one of my students left a perfect apple on the desk of one his professors. The student chose this professor because he sensed that she was very unhappy in her job, and he guessed that she didn't have very many friends. The next day, the professor brought in the apple and announced to the class, "Just to let you know that I'm not falling for any of this," dropping the apple in the trash can. It was probably one of the most personally enlightening experiences my student had that entire semester—he recognized immediately the importance of keeping himself open to all the good things that come his way in the course of his ordinary day.

Regardless of people's unexpected responses, I hope that your experience with this exercise will be so much fun that it will become a regular part of your week. Perhaps you will be as well rewarded as was one of my colleagues, who invented the idea of Poetry Attack Day in her poetry class. She asked each of her poetry students to compose funny and meaningful poems and stealthily pin them on their favorite faculty members' doors in the dark of night. The next day the college was blooming with poetry, and there were smiles on faces from one end of the campus to the other. One of the groundskeepers even taped his poem to his truck's windshield. Good karma.

Acts of Loving Kindness

The ultimate defeat of anger is not more self-control. It is love. That is pretty much a slam dunk: the more you fill your heart with loving kindness, the less vulnerable your heart will be to either the physical or the spiritual pain of anger.

That was pretty much the whole point of the third journal exercise in this chapter. If you did what I hoped you would do, you ended that meditation overwhelmed with feelings of love and tenderness toward the person whose image you had held in your mind's eye. If you *really, really* did what I asked you to do, by the end of that meditation you might have noticed a few drops of salty fluid pooling around your eyeballs. You were filling your cold, angry, dark heart with the light of loving kindness.

Getting all misty-eyed isn't really getting the job done, however. You can't just *feel* loving kindness; you have to express it in a way that somebody else can feel and understand. And so, consider the meditation below.

A CONCLUDING MEDITATION: LOVING KINDNESS

Look around your home to find the person who has been having the roughest week or day. Maybe it is even the person you most recently tried to act like Moses with. Make it your pleasure to offer that person a gentle, loving massage—a back rub, a foot rub, a shoulder massage, or a neck massage. Take your time, and completely communicate your love for that person through your hands. Try to remember to repeat this exercise with as many people in your life as you can. *Experience* how it makes you feel, both during the massage and for a good long while after. It's one of the deep joys of our primate ancestry. Who knows—maybe something nice will happen to you in return!

5

The Challenge
of Acceptance

Imagine yourself taking on the following challenge: For one entire day, you cannot make any attempts to fix anything (unless you are directly asked to help someone, or unless the wheels on the car are about to fall off). You may not give any advice, and you may not offer any opinions. You may not complain or give in to the compulsion to wring the neck of someone who truly, desperately deserves it. All you can do for twenty-four hours is live your life as it unfolds.

I bet you'd feel like you were going crazy by lunchtime.

In this chapter we are going to explore the challenge of *acceptance*. I suppose I don't have any real hope of turning you into a modern-day Buddha, but I do hope to help you become more fully aware of how essential acceptance is to your ability to both stay on an even emotional keel and continue learning to master your angry impulses and feelings.

THE BASIC PHILOSOPHY OF ACCEPTANCE

The idea of acceptance doesn't require a whole lot of explanation. However, the practice of acceptance is extremely difficult. When you were six years old your mom told you it was extremely dangerous to accept candy or other gifts from strangers. If you accepted a ride home with somebody you didn't know, you were told, then you would wake up dead in a dumpster somewhere. Somehow, by the time you were a teenager you had figured out that accepting favors and assistance could really complicate your life, and you also learned that people who accepted help were often weak and ineffectual "pussies."

Later on, you learned that if you accepted everything that grown-ups told you (such as whom to hang out with, what clothes to wear, and what beliefs to hold), your life would be far more complicated. But you also learned that being accepted by the other kids at school, and being accepted on the team, and getting accepted into college or the marines was a really important goal. If you are gay you probably learned that being accepted as straight was important for your survival. And if you didn't want to be laughed at, you also had to accept that you really sucked at some things, and that you needed to accept the necessity of avoiding those things as much as possible.

But then there were all the things you learned not to accept. You learned not to accept being disrespected, and you learned the importance of not accepting any bullshit from someone if you had a halfway decent chance of taking them on in a fight. If you were like most adolescent males you learned not to accept any criticism from your girlfriend, at least not in public. You learned that real men don't accept defeat, and real men don't accept their physical limitations.

You learned to accept a beer or a joint or a dare from any idiot who offered one to you. If you played football, you learned to accept pain; if you wrestled, you learned to accept the necessity of starving yourself before weigh-ins. If your goal was to get into a really good college, you learned to accept the loneliness of being a "brainiac"; if you are of an ethnic minority, you learned to accept that the world is full of racists; if you were gay, you learned to accept the constant fear of being beaten up without warning.

There was probably a time when you learned the importance of accepting another guy's deep friendship, and at one time you may have even been able to accept the idea that a really wonderful person loved you as a human being. As you have gotten older, you've probably had to accept the reality that people close to you will die, and that love itself can die if it is not nurtured and cherished. You may have started to accept that you're getting older and balder, and (if you have teenagers) more stupid. If you're reading this book, you have accepted that you have a problem with anger.

In this chapter we'll focus on two realities that a lot of people, especially angry men, have enormous trouble accepting. The first is your imperfect self, and the second is our imperfect world.

WORKING TOWARD SELF-ACCEPTANCE

Americans tend to be fixated on the problem of self-esteem. Perhaps the reason for this is that our self-esteem, the way we privately think about and evaluate who we really are, is overly determined by what other people think of us. Other people's opinions are important, of course, but you can't spend your entire day worrying about whether you are good enough in the eyes of other people. If you rely too much on what others think about you, then your self-esteem will be constantly rising and falling like the stock market on a busy afternoon.

I'm afraid that our culture has done a pretty terrible job at helping kids find a solid ethical basis, within themselves, of establishing their self-esteem. It seems perfectly natural to us that just about everyone around us has a say in our self-esteem. Fashion editors, schoolteachers, Little League coaches, Sunday school teachers, and beauty pageant judges all claim a chunk of the self-esteem of the young people they influence. Because we have so little control over our own self-acceptance we become consumed with worry about whether we are really worth anything. The result is a permanent self-esteem crisis in our nation. Turn on the television and you will see hundreds of commercials offering us things we can buy to bolster our faltering sense of self-worth. You can buy stuff to make your erections bigger so you can amaze your sexual partner, you can buy stuff to poison the weeds in your lawn so your neighbors will respect you, and you can demonstrate that you know the best way to ship packages and get a good deal on paper clips so you can impress your boss.

If you ignore all these messages, you will probably find yourself in the loser lane on the expressway of American life. Face it, a guy with your bad hair, yellow teeth, offensive body odor, wimpy car, bad taste in beer, flabby abdomen, meager erection, and inability to plan a fun family vacation just isn't going to cut it in today's world. The advertising industry takes it as a given that your ability to accept yourself for who and what you are is nil.

No wonder a culture so obsessed with the self-esteem of children produces so many insecure adults. Whatever the cause of this phenomenon, plenty of psychologists agree that by the time most Americans reach adulthood they have been successfully persuaded that they aren't much good.

The Self-Esteem of Men

Men and women manifest the consequences of unstable self-esteem in different ways. In men, inadequate self-esteem manifests itself most visibly through anger. Anger often arises in direct proportion to the amount of threat a situation poses to a man's self-confidence, probably because of something related to perceived responsibility and assignment of blame. Say, for example, something's gone wrong at work. Let's look at two work-related scenarios to see how this might play out. In scenario A, you are certain that you bear no responsibility for the problem—the problem was definitely caused by someone else. In scenario B, you know that you should accept at least some responsibility for the problem—perhaps you didn't give clear instructions, failed to provide adequate supervision, or actually made a mistake. In scenario A, you will probably be able to assess the situation neutrally, without feeling defensive, and you will not become angry. In scenario B, on the other hand, the emotions you experience are much more likely to turn into anger and get you even deeper in trouble.

Male self-esteem is very much on the line in almost every situation. Others expect us, and we expect ourselves, to be competent, responsible, and effective each and every time we are at bat. It is almost as if the entire edifice of self-esteem has to be rebuilt every single day when we get out of bed. We know that we are being judged for every screwup, and we know that people are not only watching but also keeping score. For most of us, there is precious little "self" in our self-esteem, because we believe that others' perceptions of us are more important than our own self-perceptions. Even after a hundred nearly perfect performances, one failed performance can knock down the entire edifice of our self-worth—especially when we know that we are responsible for messing up.

Self-Esteem and Self-Acceptance

One of the great things about practicing mindfulness is that it enables us to be successful more often (and screw up less) simply by being aware of what we are doing moment by moment. This harkens back to the idea of *flow*, which we encountered earlier in this book. Centered, mindful people are more likely to experience flow, and they are less likely to let transient emotions and situational pressures mess them up. An even more profound benefit from practicing mindfulness, however, is that it casts a bright light on the connection between self-esteem and self-acceptance.

To put it most simply, after you have practiced mindfulness for a while you will be able to see that externally based self-esteem is pretty much a trap that you don't have to fall into. Once you have begun to comprehend that your worth as a human being really doesn't need to vary from day to day based on the latest reports about what the world thinks of you, you will realize a great boost in your freedom.

Once you are able to consistently ignore the complex apparatus you have been using all these years to receive the latest appraisals of your masculinity, power, and vulnerabilities, you are out from under an enormous weight. And once you are out from under that weight you are a whole lot freer than you were before. Of course, that still leaves you with the issue of self-acceptance, but at least now you know who you are up against.

The Struggle for Self-Acceptance

As you start to understand that other people cannot control your evaluation of yourself, you ought to find far fewer excuses to walk around being angry at everyone. But that doesn't let you off the hook, of course, with your most persistent and harshest critic—yourself. So, although experiencing this realization is a big step, it probably hasn't addressed the problem of the deepest and most disturbing source of criticism in your life.

There are at least three reasons why you are still the head critic of your own life:

1. You are still an imperfect being. There are still a lot of areas in your life where you can make some major improvements,

and, as we'll see in a later chapter, there are probably a lot of people you still need to improve your relationship with.

2. You have undoubtedly internalized an awful lot of truly bad ideas about the way you *should* behave and *ought* to live your life. Most of these bad ideas are ones you accepted and internalized during adolescence, when you felt that you needed to prove your manhood in the face of every possible challenge. You probably picked up a whole lot of bad ideas from your dad (who probably no longer feels the need to live by them himself anymore!), and if you had an angry coach or two, you probably internalized a lot of his nonsense as well.

3. Most important, you have relatively little idea how to do self-acceptance. Almost none of the men I work with are able to give themselves a pat on the back or pay themselves a compliment.

Journal Exercise 5-1: It's Okay to Be Okay

Ouch! This is going to hurt. This journal exercise asks you to inventory the things about yourself that are good, worthy, impressive, and exceptional. This should be the list of your attributes and qualities that you hope that your children get from you, and that you hope they would take pride in possessing. Do not stop, do not eat, and do not sleep until you have come up with at least a dozen great human qualities that you possess. Then write them down in your journal.

Now it's time to do something a little harder. Stare at your own eyes in the mirror for at least three whole minutes. When the three minutes are up, add a few more items to your list.

Next comes one of the most difficult exercises in this entire book: sit down with your spouse or partner (or your best friend, if you don't have a partner), and ask that person to tell you what items she or he would put on the list of your best and most worthy attributes. Add all these items to your list.

Analyzing Your Positive Attributes

One of the first things you probably noticed about completing this exercise is how difficult, unnatural, and even embarrassing it is to say anything nice about yourself. That discomfort is simply a reflection of the training you've received since you were small, which taught you that "good people" never, ever brag about themselves. And you have learned not only to avoid bragging about yourself but even to avoid having positive thoughts about yourself. No matter how full of perfectionism, compulsiveness, manly stoicism, and perseverance you are, there's simply no chance that you walk around every day thinking positive thoughts about who you are as a human being. The culture just won't let us do it!

But take a close look at your list. What do you see? I suspect you will see a person who, in fact, is a pretty decent human being. I am almost certain you are going to see a person who really hopes that his kids want to possess a whole lot of his positive traits. I also expect that you did *not* include anything on your list about being a hot-tempered, angry S.O.B., so I hope you can see the disconnect between the man of quality and virtue that you want to be and the angry tyrant that you find yourself being from time to time.

Scoring Your Manhood

Every man has his own opinions about which attributes define a man as being of good character and virtue. In this exercise you'll find a list of twelve qualities that African-American men most admire in a man, according to the research of psychologists Wizdom Hammond and Jacqueline Mattis (2005). While your own list might be different from theirs, these attributes provide a good starting point for thinking about how you evaluate yourself as a man. Take a look at their list, and honestly rate yourself on a scale of 0 ("This is not at all important to my definition of manhood") to 6 ("This is extremely important to my definition of manhood") on each of the qualities given.

1. A man is responsible and accountable. _____

2. A man exercises authority over himself. _____

3. A man provides for his family. _____

4. A man acknowledges his spirituality. _____

5. A man has strong morals, is upright. _____

6. A man's family is at the core of his life. _____

7. A man is concerned about personal growth. _____

8. A man demonstrates leadership and helps others.
    _____

9. A man is grounded, demonstrates stability. _____

10. A man receives and gives respect. _____

11. A man serves his community. _____

12. A man strives to overcome hardships. _____

Your Score _____

Well, there you have it—perhaps the first test of your manhood that didn't involve taking your clothes off, using a ruler for any purpose, or threatening to harm yourself or someone else. But how did you do?

The maximum possible score is 72. If you are a superhero, your score might be a little over 60. If you rated yourself as just average, your score would be around 40.

There are two points to be made about this. The first is that if your score is low (remember, this is by your own standards), then you can start doing something about it right now. The second is that if you really want to enjoy authentic self-acceptance, then you probably need to explore ways that you can increase your score.

Journal Exercise 5-2: Building Self-Acceptance

A few additional qualities appeared on Hammond and Mattis's list, including items related to self-awareness, protecting the family, and being emotionally available to others. You, too, may have thought of additional items that aren't on their list.

In this journal exercise, your task is to first carefully assess your score on the quiz, then score yourself on any additional items you may have thought of, and then make a list of the three or four qualities that you would really like to focus on in order to improve your own manhood score.

After you have identified those three or four qualities, take some time to meditate on why you value these particular aspects of manhood. Think about how you can go from just thinking about them to actually engaging them in an active and deliberate way in your everyday life.

Back to Self-Acceptance

I hope you can appreciate the radical shift that this chapter is proposing in the way you think about and go about achieving self-acceptance. Let's review where we've been so far.

The first thing we did was to separate your self-esteem from other people's perceptions of you. Then we decided that, because all too often self-esteem rises and falls artificially on the tide of short-term outcomes and current events, it is not a valuable guide for how to live your life.

That realization shifted our focus to the longer-term issue of self-acceptance. I tried to get you to see how deeply engrained our fear of self-acceptance is in our culture, and that true self-acceptance is grounded in how well you actually live up to the standards and ideals that you have set for yourself as a man. And, of course, you discovered that even by your own standards you are sometimes less than the ideal person you aim to be. Being slightly imperfect simply makes you human and perhaps gives us all some things to kid you about. Imperfection is a fact of life, but it does not need to fuel the anger that is making you even more imperfect.

Finally, you considered deliberate approaches you could take that would grant you the right to live your life with a higher level of legitimate self-acceptance.

If the anger control experts out there are even partially correct about the important link between anger and the vulnerability of a man's self-respect system, then the best cure for your anger really lies deeply in the core of your *character* as a man and a human being. And once again we come to the conclusion that the issue isn't about learning how to *control* your anger; the issue is about how you live your life.

ACCEPTING THE WORLD

This chapter began with the assertion that there are two aspects of acceptance that play a part in our study of anger. We've discussed the challenge of accepting our imperfect selves; now we'll look at acceptance of the world, which is also a difficult proposition.

The Man in the Hole

As you read the parable below, developed by Dr. Steven Hayes and his colleagues (1999) at the University of Nevada in Reno, try to put yourself in the poor fellow's place.

A parachutist once dropped from an airplane in the middle of the night, landing in the middle of a vast, treeless field far away from any evidence of human habitation. He passed out when he hit the ground, and when he came to he got to his feet and stumbled around in the dark looking for any source of light that he could head toward. After taking a few steps in the pitch dark the man walked right into a vertical wall of dirt. He fell down, picked himself up, and walked a few feet in the opposite direction. Once again he walked into a vertical wall of dirt. The man had landed in a hole; when he looked up he could see just the faintest trace of some stars, and he realized that he had fallen into a very, very deep hole indeed.

The man took off his backpack and felt around inside it. The pack was empty, but for one tool, his trusty folded trenching shovel. The man assembled the shovel and immediately went to work digging furiously all the rest of the night. By the time the sun finally rose, the man had dug himself down an additional three feet. Exhausted, the man collapsed into a deep sleep where he dreamed that by some miracle he had discovered a very large

*steam shovel in the bottom of his hole. But when he awoke,
he realized he had only been dreaming and sadly went back to
working with his little shovel, making his hole deeper, inch by
inch—trying all the time not to think about how hopeless his
situation really was.*

While you are thinking about what a mess our poor parachutist is in, I'll tell you another story about a man in a jam. This story is also adapted from a tale by Steve Hayes and his sadistic friends in Nevada as part of their approach to acceptance and commitment therapy (ACT).

The Tug-of-War with the Monster

*The following events took place many years ago, in the same
treeless field where our parachutist is now struggling for his life.
The hole was already quite deep in those days, and it was tended
by a very strong and very fierce monster (in a red hat, if that
makes any difference). Because he had lost a bet over how many
pieces of apple pie he could eat in thirty minutes, a man, the hero
of our tale, was compelled to get into a tug-of-war competition
with the monster as a test of his manly strength. The battle took
place on either side of the hole, with the monster on one side and
the man on the other.*

  *The man was quite strong, but the monster was very strong
as well. The monster pulled, and the man pulled back. This went
on all day and all night, and the man was getting increasingly
tired. As his muscles became exhausted the man weakened and
grew desperately afraid he was going to lose the tug-of-war and
get pulled into the pit. He cried out to heaven for help from his
god, but all that came back was a single piece of advice.*

Now, here's where it starts to get interesting. What was the heavenly advice? If you want to get a man's opinion about what the advice was, ask your sons or any other young men in your life. If you want to *know* what the advice was, ask your wife or partner.

And now, while you are worrying about the man in the hole and the man about to get pulled into the hole, here's a third story. This is an ancient teaching story that has probably been around as long as the monster in the red hat.

The Unlucky, Feckless Robin

There once was a lazy robin who delayed his preparations for his southern migration until winter was just around the corner. One night, while he was asleep, a freezing rain fell, and the robin's wings froze shut. The half-frozen robin fell out of his tree in a feathery mass, and he would have died, but, as luck would have it, just as he was falling an old cow wandered under the tree and deposited a great big hot cow pie. The feckless, half-frozen robin landed in the cow pie, and its heat thawed him completely. The little robin was saved! He was so happy that he wiggled out of the cow pie. But then, realizing that he was now covered from beak to tail in cow manure, he began sounding great angry cries. Just then the farmer's cat wandered by and heard the robin's cries. Being a cat, he went over and promptly ate the robin.

The Morals of These Tales?

Well, let's take them in reverse order. The morals of the story about the robin are as follows: First, you ought to do what you are supposed to do when you are supposed to do it. Second, you never know who is going to happen along and save your life at any given moment. Third, if you find yourself covered in shit, but warm and still alive, it is probably best to keep your mouth shut about it.

The morals of the tale about the tug-of-war with the monster? First, you probably shouldn't make any bets that you can't afford to lose. Second, *drop the rope.*

And the morals of the story about the man in the hole? First, I'm awful glad it's not me. Second, I don't have a clue—but I am pretty sure that the answer isn't to keep digging!

The story about the robin may or may not be just a joke. But the other two stories are definitely not. I have met very few men and boys under the age of twenty-five who can solve that tug-of-war problem. They invariably offer solutions that include inventing a tree, a bulldozer, or a weapon. Almost none can accept the wisdom of dropping the rope.

Frankly, nobody does very well in solving the man-in-the-hole story. Angry people say that the answer is to get angry; depressed people think the answer is to just lie at the bottom of the thing and wait to die. Anxious people get claustrophobic and expect the earth to cave in around them. I suppose the truly religious just wait to be rescued. But just about everybody can figure out to stop digging—unless and until it is them in the bottom of that hole.

The message of all three stories is that there are a great many problems in this world that require us to come to terms with *acceptance*. Clearly that's the lesson the robin and the man involved in the tug-of-war should have learned. Accepting that you can't win every tug-of-war and that sometimes you need to just drop the rope is pretty obvious, once somebody says it to you. But does the man in the hole need to accept?

Well, I guess you need to accept that your trusty shovel won't be able to get you out of every fix you find yourself in. Eventually you have to accept that no matter how skillful you are you may not have the right tools to fix your situation. You might need to accept that you are just going to have to wait until someone comes along with a ladder. But mostly you have to accept that, for the moment, you are fresh out of good ideas about how to turn things around.

Beyond Acceptance

While we're still thinking about how the parachutist might get himself out of that hole, I'd like to point out that there is a substantial difference between acceptance and surrender. Your mindfulness practice should not lead you to embrace fatalism where, like the depressed guy in the hole, you just sit around waiting to die. The acceptance that comes with mindfulness is a calming, thoughtful, and aware state of mind that is conducive to acting effectively when opportunity is present.

If you have spent a lot of time in big holes in the past you would undoubtedly have a very different response to your predicament than you had the first time it happened to you. Perhaps all holes are pretty much alike, or maybe an experienced hole dweller recognizes all sorts of subtle differences in the ground materials, the angle of the sides, and the places where they hide the escape tunnels in most big holes.

Mindfulness makes it possible for you to explore the inherent possibilities in your situation and harnesses your creative energies, using those brain cells in your right prefrontal cortex to your maximum advantage. By accepting the significance and the gravity of his situation with mindful attention, the hole dweller can focus on three crucial tasks before him.

1. He can explore his *goals*. I'm not a terribly competent home-repair guy, but I get a big kick out of trying. So I keep a poster over the workbench in my garage that reads "It is difficult to remember that your objective was to drain the swamp when you are up to your ass in alligators." Keeping your eye on the goal when everything seems to be going to hell in a handbasket can be a really tough proposition. If you are so pissed off at or intimidated by the alligators that you can't keep track of your mission, then you are unlikely to make much progress with the water level in the swamp. Mindfulness is an extraordinarily important tool for keeping your mind focused clearly on your true goals.

2. He can be fully aware of his *pathways*. Western psychologists help many of their clients out of difficult situations by encouraging them to carefully consider what workable solutions they already have available to them that can put them on a pathway toward achieving their goals (Snyder, Michael, and Cheavens 1999). In Buddhist philosophy the term for this is *skillful means* (performing a task in a practiced, smooth, skillful, and efficient way), which involves more than just knowing what to do. It implies doing what you are doing both with focused *effort* and with a grace that allows you to achieve your goal with a minimum of fuss, bother, and wasted motion.

3. He can make a solemn *commitment*. This idea of commitment harkens back to chapter 1 in this book, and the idea of becoming the hero of your own life. To accomplish one's goals, and to stay firmly on one's chosen path without excuses, without wavering, and without compromise, one must make a commitment. It means accepting responsibility for persevering toward your goals, regardless of how frustrating, boring, or difficult it may be.

The purpose of the following exercise is to give you an opportunity to put these ideas into practice. By starting small you will have the opportunity to see how mindful practice can be applied to other situations in your life, particularly those that you find frustrating and difficult to accomplish without the interference of doubt and anger.

Journal Exercise 5-3:
A Small Bit of Perfection

Begin by selecting an ordinary task that you perform on a regular basis, preferably daily. This could be anything from packing your kids' lunches to brushing your teeth or greeting the people in your office. The task should be one that you perform automatically, without much thought, but one that you could perfect if you paid attention to what you were doing.

Establish a meaningful goal that you could realistically achieve, for example, "I'll perfectly sort each day's mail when I come home from work," "I'll clean the kitchen every night after dinner until every surface is shining," or "I'll make the time to talk to each of my kids for at least five uninterrupted minutes about something they are interested in, at least three times a week."

Figure out a practical pathway you can follow in order to reach this goal, such as making sure you have on hand the materials you need to make those lunches or clean the stove, or making sure you arrive at the office early enough every day to have time to greet everyone by name.

Make a commitment to follow your pathway to reach your goal every day for at least two full weeks. Accept responsibility for doing it without delays, excuses, or half-measures.

In your journal, keep a record of the thing you've decided to perfect in your life. Every day, note how successful you were in living up to your commitment. Take a close look at your excuse system, and see if you can find some way of strengthening your determination to take charge of your own life.

Acceptance of an Imperfect World

It probably hasn't escaped your attention that we live in an imperfect world. A lot of the goods and services you buy are pretty inferior, and a lot of the people you have to deal with on a regular basis could be a lot smarter, more helpful, and less unpleasant to work with.

Your kids could be more respectful, your partner could be more appreciative, your dog could learn to poop someplace other than the middle of the front lawn. Of course the fact that you, yourself, are pretty imperfect doesn't make life any easier either.

The life goal of virtually all of the angry men I know is to reform the rest of the world. They seem to believe that their mission on the planet is to point out and correct everyone's mistakes, no matter how many hours are lost in the process and how much unhappiness they create in the process.

Given the number of angry people running around in the world, you might reasonably expect that just about all the mistakes would have been corrected by now and all the incorrect people would have been reformed four times over. But somehow the world is still imperfect, and nobody seems to be able to do a damned thing about it.

As with all the other bewildering problems that beset us humans, the problem of imperfection is one that Buddhist thinkers have been puzzling over for centuries. Their logical conclusion, unfortunately, is that imperfection is an inescapable part of the human condition, but that our response to imperfection is something that can be the focus of our meditation.

My friend and colleague Maurits Kwee (1996) has collected a number of stories about imperfection, and the acceptance of imperfection, that are worth retelling.

THE TENNIS MATCH

A priest and a nun were once playing a game of tennis. The nun played with excellent skill, but the priest often missed the ball or hit it out of bounds. Each time he missed, he exclaimed, "Damn it, I missed!" And each time, the nun became upset and in an angry tone of voice asked him to stop cursing. The priest promised he would try harder not to curse anymore and offered the prayer, "Lord, if I cannot stop cursing, punish me with lightning and turn me into ashes." The game continued. But then the priest missed a very easy shot and impulsively shouted, "Damn it, I missed!" Immediately the sky darkened, thunder clouds appeared, and lightning flashed downward. The nun took a direct hit and was changed into a pile of ash. Just then a voice roared down from heaven, "Damn it, I missed!"

The following story is a traditional Buddhist tale.

THE MONKS AND THE MAIDEN

A senior monk and a young novice were walking along a mountain path one day when they came to a river with no bridge across it. They took off their sandals and were about to cross to the other side when they heard a young woman softly sobbing under a tree. They went over to the tree and asked the young woman what the problem was, and she explained that she was traveling to visit her sick grandmother who lived on the other side of the mountain, but that the river was so high and the current so strong she feared she could not cross to the other side without drowning. The old priest held out his arm and said that he would happily carry the young woman across the river on his back.

Despite the young novice's objections, because they had both taken a monastic vow of chastity (which forbade any physical contact with women), the monk carried the woman across the river, and once they were across the two holy men and the woman went their separate ways. That night over their dinner at an inn, the young novice was visibly angry. When the monk asked him what was troubling him, the novice hotly replied that the monk had disgraced their holy order by touching a woman, and he could no longer respect him as his teacher.

The old monk looked the young man in the eye and said, "Grasshopper, it is you who have sinned. For I put the woman down after carrying her but a few yards across the river. But you are still carrying her."

What is the cause of the angry suffering in these two stories? A Buddhist would tell you that it was not caused by the priest's cursing or the monk's bending of his vows. It was caused by a lack of acceptance of imperfection. Since every living thing is connected imperceptibly but profoundly to every other living thing on the planet, it is, in essence, impossible for us to point the finger of blame at any one person, event, or time as the absolute source of imperfection. The only rational, sensible, and humane thing we can do is to *accept* that imperfection exists, and to commit ourselves to minimizing its impact on the rest of the world.

Acceptance, Causation, and Anger

Here is another story from Maurits Kwee that will make you think and smile simultaneously.

ON THE DIFFERENCE BETWEEN HEAVEN AND HELL

A very old man died who had wasted his life as an angry tyrant and thus was required to spend some time in hell. As he was wandering about, he came across an old friend, also a very old man, who was sitting with a gorgeous, sexy lady on his knee. The grumpy old man greeted his friend and exclaimed, "Surely there is some mistake. You can't truly be in a hell with a gorgeous babe like that sitting on your knee. You are having much too good a time." His friend smiled, and replied, "Oh, this is hell, all right. You see, I am her punishment!"

One man's hell is another man's heaven. It's all a matter of perspective, wisdom, and, above all, acceptance. How much better life is when you are not compelled to track down the origins of every wrong and disgraceful act that you encounter as you stumble through life. By accepting that imperfection is part of the human condition, you might even be able to take a break from your responsibility to fix every wrong that other people have committed. This break just might enable you to begin distinguishing between the things that you can change, and the things that you can't change and perhaps don't need changing anyway.

A CONCLUDING MEDITATION: JOY

Let's conclude this chapter with a meditation by the French writer André Gide (1869–1951), who wrote, "Know that joy is rarer, more difficult and more beautiful than sadness. Once you make this all-important discovery, you must embrace joy as a moral obligation."

As you meditate on this quote, you might try asking yourself how you could take on the responsibility of creating some small measure of joy in this world. Accept responsibility for making the world a little better, not just by battling against the bad and the wrong, but by adding to the joy in your children's and your partner's lives. How can you make this impulse a part of the daily practice of your existence as a human being, and thereby move forward in discovering the great depths of your own true nature?

6

Obligation: *Sumanai!*

Imagine walking up to an angry guy in a bar and asking him if he remembered to thank the bartender for serving him his last round. That probably wouldn't be a very smart thing to do, yet this chapter is going to do something like just that. We are going to work on the difficult trick of converting resentments into gratitude, and selfish preoccupation into active awareness of your debts to the people around you. You may find this to be a difficult task, so get ready to open your mind and pay attention!

SEETHING RESENTMENTS RULE!

One of the most curious things about angry people is that they tend to see themselves as the world's biggest victims. If you were asked to talk about your relationship with your supervisor at work, chances are that you would not begin by talking about how hard she works, how devoted she is to the success of the mission of your employer, or how tough her job is. You'd probably be even less likely to recount in faithful detail all of the favors and kindnesses that she has done for you over the years.

For some strange reason, we all spend a great deal of time harboring, rehearsing, and ruminating on our resentments, and we spend remarkably little time and energy thinking about, let alone acknowledging, the good and nice things that others have done for us. If you can bring yourself to mindfully begin to change this about yourself, you will experience the world in a remarkably different way.

This morning before I went to work I ran some errands: I made a deposit at the bank, I got my watch strap repaired at the jewelry store, I filled out some forms at the post office, and I stopped at the grocery store to replace an olive oil container that I had broken last night while I was cooking dinner. None of these events (except perhaps having had to mop up half a pint of olive oil) was in the least way remarkable. Nothing happened to make me angry, frustrated, or vengeful. Had I not been thinking all weekend about the concepts in this chapter I probably would not have noticed any of the following:

- The bank employee greeted me pleasantly, as if my arrival at that moment was all she really needed to have a great day.

- The jewelry store owner fixed my watch for free and reminded me to try to eat lunch outside today because the weather was perfect.

- The postal clerk greeted me by name and asked about my travel plans, since I was stopping my mail for a few days.

- The store was stocked with many choices for my olive oil container, and the checkout person admired my selection.

- The guys mowing the grass around my office stopped their machines to say hello and wish me a good day.

- The first e-mail message I opened was from a student who was thanking me for a great learning experience in a course I had taught this semester.

In contrast, I could have paid attention to a whole host of unpleasant things: arriving at my office late because the bank doesn't open until 9:00; having to repair an annoying, high-maintenance watch strap yet again; waiting in line in the post office behind people who acted like they have never purchased a stamp before; being unable to find an oil jar as big as the one I broke; hearing the constant racket generated by the lawn mowers outside my window; and—well, even I can't think of a reason to be grumpy about my student Tim's kind thank-you, but you get the point, I'm sure.

MAKING REAL CHOICES

Unless you happen to be completely alone on a deserted island, you are compelled to interact with other people all throughout your day. In a lot of these interactions you are either receiving a service or providing one to someone else, and most of the time you will judge those interactions almost exclusively in terms of their degree of unpleasantness. You will rarely think about them as opportunities to help someone else have a better day, and even less often will you think about them as small kindnesses that other people undertake to help you have a good day. It is important to note, however, that every interaction you have with a living thing creates a significant opportunity for you to have a positive influence on the world.

Paying Attention

It begins with an initial choice about your attention. I'll admit that I am such a type A, time-conscious person that most of the time I pay a good deal of attention to the task itself, and especially to the time it has consumed. But I have other choices. I can make a conscious decision about where I direct my attention. I could pay attention to the process, noticing the skill and care that the person I am dealing with is exercising in the performance of his or her duties. I noted, for example, that Tim wrote me his note at 6:20 P.M. on Saturday night, which made me realize that on his first completely free Saturday night since he started college Tim sat down at his computer and wrote me a thank-you note. What was I doing at 6:20 on Saturday night? I certainly wasn't thinking about my students and appreciating the hard work they had all put in over the course of the semester.

It is great fun to watch people engage in *skillful means* (which means, as you will recall from chapter 5, behavior that is practiced, smooth, skillful, and efficient), and I think most generally appreciate an attentive and discerning audience. This is especially true if the audience acknowledges their admiration with a compliment and a small moment of recognition.

A second choice related to attention is to really notice the person you are interacting with. The bank employee was cheerful, attentive, and very professional in the way she handled my request. Even though she has to perform the same type of transaction dozens of times a day and must come home from work some nights bored out of her mind, she really did act like helping me out was a pleasure (as did the jeweler, the postal clerk, and the store employee). If I had been at the top of my form I would have given each of these people a smile, looked them in the eye for at least a second, and offered a rather emphatic "Thank you. You've been really nice to me."

In his book on Japanese Naikan therapy, Gregg Krech (2002) (whose many valuable ideas are scattered throughout this chapter) challenges us to become masters of the perfect thank-you, which is a form of paying attention to the person you're interacting with. He suggests, for example, that we *always* acknowledge the services of others with a complete statement that mentions what the person has done for us. So, instead of simply saying "Thank you" to the jewelry store owner, I should have said, "Thank you for doing such a nice job fixing my watch strap!" This tiny addition to your routine is certain to bring a little bit of happiness to each person you are dealing with, because it shows that you aren't just on automatic pilot and really noticed the service you have received. Most of the impact of your perfect thank-you, however, will be on you, because it teaches you to focus your attention on yourself in your interactions with others. This idea, which is the focus of this chapter, may sound a little crazy at first, but I encourage you to hear it out.

One of the main reasons you have an anger problem is that your attention is significantly misdirected. If you are like me, your attention is focused on time, and your frustration threshold pretty much determines the emotional quality of the events in your life. *If* nobody messes up, *if* everybody does their job efficiently and correctly, *if* everybody minds their own business, *then* we will have a good day, and everything will be sunshine and flowers. But if my colleagues don't clear the paper jam in the copier, if my students start whining about their grades, if my spouse notices a layer of olive oil all over the kitchen floor, *then* we will definitely not have such a nice day. *If* nobody ever screwed up, *if* nobody was ever critical of my work, *if* everybody realized how important *my time* is—well, the world would be a piece of cake.

But, the copier is *always* jammed (or so it seems). I fear I didn't do a really great job of getting the olive oil mopped up. Students seem to *enjoy* complaining about their grades. And the traffic lights in this town seem to be diabolically programmed to make sure that I have to stop at every single intersection, which seriously wastes my time. So guess where my attention is!

The alternative, besides paying attention to the people and processes all around us and perfecting the art of saying thank you, is to turn your attention inward—to all of the great and wonderful things that are happening to you and for you all the time. If you try this, what you will discover is that an enormous amount of the chronic suffering we experience every day of our lives is by and large an artifact of misdirected attention. We consistently and perversely let our own self-ish desires and motives seize our well-being and destroy it. Gregg Krech illustrates this point with a story from the life of the late Mahatma Gandhi.

GANDHI'S ATTENTION

Gandhi's enemies were forever trying to kill him, so he lived most of his political life under the constant threat of assassination. One time a would-be assassin joined a large crowd that had gathered to hear Gandhi speak. The assassin intended to rush forward at some point during the speech and shoot the great man at close range. But something very strange happened. The assassin listened to Gandhi's speech about nonviolence and the struggle for equality and freedom, and his heart was changed.

At the end of Gandhi's speech the man rushed forward and, instead of trying to shoot him, confessed his plan and begged for Gandhi's forgiveness. Gandhi looked into the man's face and asked him, "But what will happen to you now that you have failed in your mission? What kind of trouble will you be in?"

Gandhi's attention, at that significant moment in his life, turned not to his close brush with death, but to the problems of his would-be assassin!

The story leads me to wonder how my obvious impatience at the post office affected the (pretty incompetent) people ahead of me in line. How did it affect the postal worker, who was trying to help every single customer with the same grace that she eventually showed me? How much suffering am I habitually creating in situations like this just because I think my time is so incredibly important?

Note, please, the result of this shift in attention. By becoming mindfully aware of the buildup of my frustration, I had the opportunity to pay attention to the effects my frustration was having on others. As a result, in a situation like this I not only have the opportunity to make life a little more pleasant for others, I actually save myself from experiencing an unreasonable and unnecessary angry episode.

The advantages of behaving mindfully in daily life are pretty obvious. Not only would mindful attention have restored my sanity, but it also would have allowed me to remember to offer a sincere thank-you to the postal clerk, graciously hold the door open for the person coming in to the post office with an armload of packages, and get to my office without my blood pressure spiking.

Journal Exercise 6-1: Thank-You Meditation

The purpose of this exercise is to help you train your attention toward the hundreds of small things that you would be grateful about, if you were paying proper attention.

Over the next twenty-four hours, write down every single thing that someone else does for you that you should be thankful for. Actually, you can't realistically do this—your list would be longer than this chapter. So settle for something like one example per waking hour until this time tomorrow. Describe each event in a complete sentence.

- Tom made coffee for everyone in the break room this morning.

- The parking lot attendant (whose name I need to learn) asked me about my weekend.

- My son cleaned up his breakfast dishes today without having to be asked.

- The server gave me a refill on my iced tea at lunch today without my asking.

Next, record how you responded to each of these events—and how you could have responded even more positively and assertively.

Finally, take careful note of how you felt after you (1) recognized the kindness that had been done, (2) graciously recognized the act with thanks, and (3) added it to your list of all the other good things that have happened to you recently.

Heaven and Hell, Revisited

Once upon a time there was a very hot-tempered and impatient young man who had been raised in a very religious home. A student of meditation, he was quite uncomfortable about the many differences between the religious teachings he had grown up with and the spiritual ideas he encountered in his meditation classes. In addition, he was becoming increasingly frustrated that, although he had spent a zillion hours sitting in mindful meditation counting his breaths, he still had not experienced even the beginning insights that come with enlightenment.

One day he couldn't stand it any longer, so he grabbed a sword and went to his teacher's room to demand that the old man resolve his vexing theological uncertainties for him. He barged into the room without knocking and demanded that the old monk explain the Buddha's ideas about heaven and hell, and do it quickly. The old monk looked at the angry youth and said, "Alas, you are too ignorant, closed minded, and full of nonsense to understand any of that. Now go away, and leave me alone."

The young man became enraged by what his teacher said to him. He drew his sharpened sword and was about to bring it down sharply on the monk's bald head. At that moment, the old man looked him in the face, smiled, and said, "Behold the gates of hell."

Upon hearing this, the young man dropped the sword and fell to his knees, thanking his teacher for this wisdom and tearfully begging for forgiveness. Once again the old man looked him in the eye, and this time he said, "Behold the gates of heaven."

And with that, the young man experienced enlightenment!

If anger is our daily hell, then surely gratitude must be our heaven. But we surely need not threaten with swords or behave imprudently (especially to our teachers) to find our way from the depths of hell to the gates of salvation.

One of my students experienced just such a transformation after spending a couple of weeks engaged in the random acts of kindness exercise you tried in chapter 4. Joel had discovered all sorts of interesting things about himself and his fraternity brothers from his random acts of kindness, and he was curious about how he might be able to take it to the next level. I asked him to tell me the three most annoying things in his life right now. The first thing he thought of was homework—but we decided that homework was just too impersonal, and it was an unavoidable part of college life. Then he thought about his unreliable computer, but there wasn't much we could do about that either. Then he thought about his fifteen-year-old sister, who drove Joel nuts, just to show that she could. She was, Joel said, just about the brattiest little sister that any guy ever had to put up with.

So we devised a loving kindness meditation for Joel to enact with his sister. He would simply refuse to take her bait any time she tried to provoke him into an argument or a dispute. Not only that, he would respond to her brattiness with nothing but loving attention and kindness. He would try his hardest to do that for an entire weekend at home.

The results were nothing less than astonishing—for both of them. Not only did the sister have her mind blown by the transformation in her big brother, but she started acting nice to him and began helping him with chores like washing his car and doing his laundry. Joel reported in his journal that after a very short amount of time had elapsed he found himself not having to think about being nice to his sister; it came to him automatically. A year later, their relationship appears to have been totally transformed by that simple weekend experiment in human kindness. Homework and computers are still problems, of course.

Journal Exercise 6-2: Strangers Bearing Gifts

This exercise requires you to conjure up the image of a person who recently incited more than his or her fair share of anger and frustration in you (and perhaps does so frequently). Go ahead and ruminate on that for a few seconds, just to make sure that you've chosen the right person.

Next, find something in your home, or at the store, to give that person as a gift. Maybe it's a bunch of flowers from your garden, a really nice apple, a coupon for a car wash, or a homemade cookie.

Now it's time to (a) present the gift to that person in a way that shows you really mean it, and (b) say thank you to that person for some specific thing he or she does that is helpful to you.

As always, record your experience in your journal, and pay really close attention to how you felt before, during, and after going through this exercise. But that's not all. There is an additional component of this exercise. I'm betting that choosing and giving a gift and thanking him or her is going to change the way you see this annoying and frustrating person. You will notice something about him or her that you never noticed before. Write that new information down.

NAIKAN THERAPY: A LIFETIME OF OBLIGATION

In Japan every waking moment is spent in felt connection with other beings. Of course, that is generally true for us North Americans too, but we pay almost no attention to that fact. Because Japanese culture focuses on the collective aspects of the society, individuals tend to define their identities according to the groups they belong to. They therefore invest a great deal of energy in carefully monitoring, maintaining, and enhancing their relationships with other people.

When you introduce yourself to someone of roughly equivalent social status and age in North America you usually identify yourself by your occupation, your recreational interests, your place of birth. You generally try to establish some sort of connection with the person you are meeting for the first time. In Japan you introduce yourself more or less silently by exchanging business cards, and you acknowledge the connections between you with a carefully rehearsed bow. While in North America strangers talk to each other, searching for something they have in common, in Japan, those relations are all spelled out on the business card. In some sense, there are no strangers in Japan because everyone ultimately has some connection with everyone else.

The Japanese business card identifies each person's role in Japanese society. Everyone has a place, a connection, and a duty. Ultimately all those duties flow upward in a hierarchical chain of command that unites the entire country under the emperor and, in striking contrast with North American society, leaves nobody out.

One for All, and All for One?

The glue that holds Japanese society together is *giri*, the vast network of obligation that is the DNA of Japanese culture. Every person, once he or she starts school, is bound by an elaborate set of social, occupational, financial, and familial connections that define that person's identity pretty much from cradle to grave. Although the system is under attack by globalization and the rise of the multinational corporations, the ideal Japanese life is still one that is tightly woven into a seamless fabric of social relationships that will define what school your kids attend, whom they will marry, what jobs they will have, and what hobbies and sports they will engage in.

As you have probably heard, the Japanese people live in an extremely, even intensely, polite society. The train conductors bow to their passengers; schoolchildren bow to their teachers; shopkeepers bow to their customers. Every transaction is a small opera of bowing, expressing appreciation, denying that anything has been any trouble or inconvenience, asserting elaborately that an enormous service has been rendered, and finally promising that the whole process will soon be repeated with great anticipation. Going to the bank to make a deposit can take fifteen minutes and involve a half-dozen bows, receipt of a token gift, and a level of personal attention that Bill Gates probably experiences when he walks into his neighborhood bank.

So there is no room for bad-mood days in Japanese public life. You can't go to work and not bow to everyone who comes and goes; you must greet every person as if your life wasn't complete until they showed up to take their important place in the assigned order of things. Having observed university life in Japan for a couple of years, I can report that there are just as many office conspiracies, lingering resentments, long knives, and petty feuds in a Japanese university department as there are in work environments everywhere else in the world, but none of it is allowed to show, or to disrupt the smooth operation of day-to-day business.

This means that in traditional Japanese society people are expected to be absolute masters of self-control. It also means that many of them suffer from all the stress-related illnesses you might expect to find in such a tightly regulated social structure. Alcohol provides the main safety valve for Japanese men. Under the influence of alcohol they are given license to speak from their hearts and express strong feelings and opinions. The catch is that they are required to do this with the same people they work with—bosses, underlings; everyone is included in these ritual-driven, alcohol-fueled decompression sessions, which may take place several nights a week. So the relief from stress is probably more ceremonial than genuine, and the next day everyone is back to work together making the magic happen all over again.

So how do Japanese people deal with this intense pressure to be perfect all the time? Well, sadly, there is a lot of suicide. But there is also a cultural obsession with strength, resiliency, and having a "big heart" full of compassion and responsibility for the people in your web of interpersonal connections. So while the most common fear of middle-aged men in Japan is that they will literally work themselves to death, the reality is that many are incapable of taking a holiday or a vacation without feeling terribly guilty and cut off from their deepest self-identity. Most of the men I know in Japan experience a visceral dread of the prospect of retirement, because their entire identity is tied up in the relationships they have in their jobs.

Naikan Therapy to the Rescue

As you might expect, a fair number of people in Japan break down under the pressure of daily life. The same is true in our society, of course; I don't mean to imply that our extreme, John Wayne–style individualism is a healthier way to live than the Japanese approach. But the response to the breakdown of individuals is extremely different in the two cultures. In the United States the broken person typically goes to a clinic and receives treatment from a medical professional, who will often give the brain neurons a chemical boost as well as listen to the client's complex personal history. Their conversation will focus on the client's *feelings*, how those feelings came into existence, and what the client can do to start feeling better. In many ways it is a lot like confession—the goal is the restoration of the person's soul to perfect health.

In Japan, the provider is strictly interested in the *facts* of the situation. He or she has no interest in hearing a confession or chang-ing the person's brain chemistry, and in fact he or she is more likely to be a Buddhist priest than a medical or psychological doctor. The Japanese therapist's mission is to gently guide you back on to the right path. He does not try to help you "discover" this path, because he respects the fact that you have spent your entire life learning what your true path is.

Let's imagine that you are a Japanese businessperson, and your temper is causing conflict in your workplace. Because you are grumpy, dissatisfied, or petulant the work of your entire group is being disrupted. You have been warned of serious potential consequences for the company if your temper continues to disrupt the smooth flow of important work. Your boss politely asks you to talk with a counselor who can skillfully help you rejoin your team of coworkers.

So you go to the clinic, suitcase in hand because you know that your problems are quite serious and you have a great deal of work to do to get your life back in order. Depending on the nature of your problem you could be a candidate for any number of therapies (Reynolds 1980), but since your problem relates to your anger you are assigned to the Naikan therapy program.

Your therapist sees you as a person who has cracked under stress—that is, you have lost sight of what is valuable, meaningful, important, and most human about your existence. He sees your temper and your anger as your neurotic attempt to break away from the conditions that sustain you. You are weak, you are selfish, and you are deluded. You are a serious problem (note that he doesn't say you *have* a serious problem, as a Western therapist surely would). You are in extreme danger of divorcing yourself from the only force that sustains human life—your giri, your web of connection with everyone in your life. Why, you almost sound like an American!

The Naikan therapist isn't very interested in your personal reasons for being in this condition. The specific facts about your case may help predict how long it will take to restore you to your proper place in society, but your feelings about your situation are pretty irrelevant to how your treatment will proceed.

Your basic humanity needs to be jump-started. The first step in the process is to conduct a very thorough review of the facts of your life. For most people this means concentrating on the most basic relationship that exists anywhere in nature, your relationship with your mother. For several complicated cultural reasons, I don't believe that the specific example of *mother* works very well for Western clients, so for the purposes of this scenario, feel free to substitute the person who has been the most important in your life—your brother, your spouse, a living relative, or a long-lost friend. As you will soon see, it doesn't really matter all that much.

THE THREE QUESTIONS

Now that you have that person firmly in mind, you need to answer three *factual* questions about your relationship with that person, which are the first three questions in the exercise below. For convenience we will restrict the domain of these questions to the last six months. But in formal Naikan therapy you would answer each of these questions for a specified time period, such as "in your childhood," "when you were at university," "before you were married," or "after your son was born." To try your hand at Naikan, complete the following exercise.

Journal Exercise 6-3: Mining Your Naikan

You'll need to set aside at least an hour to complete this exercise. Find a time and place where you won't be interrupted, since you'll need to do this exercise without talking to anyone. This exercise will help you identify the heart of your relationship with the person who is most important to you by carefully thinking about how you are giving more back to the relationship than you are taking from it. In your journal, answer the following questions:

- What are the ten most important things you have received from the person who is most important to you? Take as much time as you need to make this list.

- What are the most valuable things that you have given in this relationship (such as loyalty, fidelity, love, honesty, money, security, joy, happiness, understanding, compassion)?

- What troubles or difficulties have you caused for that person? Make a complete inventory, using as much time as is necessary.

- How have your problems burdened this person?

- How could you have done a better job of caring for and supporting this person?

- What messages have your actions toward this person communicated? Have you let this person know how important he or she is in your life?

- What responsibility have you taken for the problems you have caused this person?

- What is it like to have you as a spouse, child, boss, father, or partner? What is it like to be married to you? What is it like to have you as a son? What is it like to have you as a dad?

Finally, mindfully meditate, with seriousness and an open heart, on your answers to these questions.

Giving Yourself Away

Gregg Krech (2002) runs the TōDō Institute, a Naikan therapy treatment center in Vermont, where you can experience the real thing with a trained staff. But I think you can accomplish a great deal at home by taking the three Naikan questions and applying them to all of your most important relationships. What you are trying to do in this exercise is to develop an outside-inside view of yourself as a human being.

That basic *factual* question, "What is it like to have me as a spouse (or son, father, partner, uncle, or friend)?" is a question that could literally change your life, for the good, forever. Notice how the question is designed to reduce suffering by changing the focus of your inquiry. You are no longer asking "Why am I an angry person?" Or even "Can I learn how to be a less angry person?" You are asking a much more profound and fundamental question: "Can I be aware of how my anger poisons the lives of the people all around me, including the people I love?"

The next logical question, then, is "Can I develop sufficient self-awareness to allow me to change my impact on the lives of my fellow human beings?" Can you recognize and appreciate the great array of gifts you have been given, starting before you were born, and are you capable of taking responsibility for the great debt that you owe because of all those gifts? Can you live your life with sincere and honest gratitude, and pass those gifts along to those who are coming along after you? If you can, then I truly think anger will cease to be a major problem in your life.

ON THE DIFFICULTY WITH BEING VIRTUOUS

Krech uncovered a little wisdom from Ben Franklin's personal diaries that I find both amusing and powerful with respect to this whole subject. Franklin, evidently, had quite a problem with practicing a number of virtues that he felt were very important for a good man to have. The toughest, he wrote, was the virtue of humility. As Franklin noted, if he ever got to the point where he had truly mastered his considerable pride and embraced a deep and genuine humility, he would almost certainly take pride in having achieved it! But the interesting thing about at least *trying* to practice humility, he observed, is that one can do a pretty good job of creating the *appearance* of it.

The same can undoubtedly be said for anger control. During the months I have spent writing this book I have become much more aware of my own anger and the things that seriously challenge my temper. Perhaps I have not really become less angry, but I believe I have created the appearance of being a less-angry person—and in many ways that is almost good enough. You probably aren't going to become the next Gandhi just because you read this book and completed the exercises. But you probably can embrace the idea that you can behave in a way that is more like the way you want people to think of you. The idea of behaving in a positive way is expressed in the oldest and most famous prayer in all of Buddhist teaching:

Always do good
Never do evil
Keep your heart pure
This is the way of the Buddha

Which brings us to a fourth journal exercise in this chapter.

Journal Exercise 6-4: Giving Yourself Away

Creating the appearance of virtue is actually a way of being virtuous. Here are a dozen activities, some of which I've adapted from Gregg Krech's book *Naikan: Gratitude, Grace, and the Japanese Art of Self-Reflection* (2002), that you can try, in order to see if you enjoy following the path of the Buddha. See how many of these you can accomplish over the next few days. Record your experiences in your journal.

- Go out of your way to make a little kid laugh.

- Go out of your way to make a big kid feel special.

- Pick up some trash that isn't in your own front yard.

- Help bag someone else's groceries; help carry them to that person's car.

- Send postcards to a bunch of people you rarely see.

- Send postcards to a bunch of people you see all the time.

- Tell somebody that you think his or her shoes are really spiffy.

- Bring a cup of coffee to a crossing guard, or someone else working outside on a cold morning.

- Double your normal tip the next time you eat out.

- Read the newspaper to somebody in a nursing home.

- Leave a big note on your garbage can that says, "Thanks, guys—you do a great job!"

- Leave a note for your mail carrier saying thanks for the great service.

OBLIGATION—SUMANAI!

One of the things that colleges drill into the heads of their students is that they aren't just getting an education, they are building a lifelong relationship with an ancient and venerable institution—that has an insatiable thirst for cold, hard cash. No matter how feckless or inept college students may be at eighteen years old, their alma mater will never forget them, and it will go to the ends of the earth to track them down at the beginning of every annual fund campaign year. A graduate can't just write a check for $10,000 and tell the college, "That's all you are going to get. Now leave me alone, forever!"

Colleges are a lot like many things in life in this respect: there is no end to our obligations, and it is difficult to escape the vast web of these obligations that we all undertake in our daily lives. As I suggested earlier in this chapter, obligation has an almost religious importance in Japan, and this leads to some interesting cultural practices.

No Thank You!

If you ever go to Japan you will learn that tipping is all but forbidden in the land of the rising sun. You would tip porters or people whom you've asked to do strange things for you, like carry a big box of books from the taxi to the post office, but otherwise tipping is considered deeply insulting in everyday life in Japan. Why? In offering a tip, you are singling someone out for doing his or her job—a job being performed in concert with untold numbers of other people. By tipping the waiter you appear to be presupposing a private master-servant relationship with him—as opposed to recognizing that the waiter is part of the highly interdependent team that began with a farmer planting some rice seeds and ended, many hundreds of transactions later, with you eating that rice.

This is a pretty cool idea, and one that cheap people like me can really appreciate. When my family and I spent time in Japan, I found that I enjoyed not to have to calculate tips and worry about who deserved what for the services they had provided. But then we slowly became aware that the no-tipping tradition was really just the tip of the cultural iceberg. As our Japanese language skills got stronger we came to realize that the only people in the entire country who actually said "please" and "thank you" in stores, restaurants, and the like were foreigners like ourselves.

Here we were in the politeness center of the world, where it took four bows to order a doughnut, but nobody was saying those "magic words" that our moms all taught us as soon as we were old enough to babble even slightly coherently. Well, it turns out that in traditional

Japanese society the word *please* has more or less the same connotation that tipping has—by saying "please," I am asking you to do me a favor or a personal service. The doughnut server is there to serve the doughnuts to everyone who honors the bakery with their business, so asking her to do her job is actually kind of insulting.

Okay, you get it, right? But what about thanking someone? Surely that wouldn't be taken the wrong way, would it? Well, that concept also turns out to be a little deeper than you might expect (as many things Japanese turn out to be). A Japanese friend, who told me about her own experience as an exchange student in the United States, said it was very hard for her to learn to say "thank you" to her friends, and especially her friends' parents. In Japan, one doesn't say "thank you" to friends and parents, one says, "Sumanai!"

Sumanai! essentially means "This is not finished!" It is a way of acknowledging and accepting an obligation that arises from accepting an act of kindness. This kind of obligation (*on* in Japanese, pronounced "own") is the building block of giri, the life-sustaining web of obligations that marks civilized human existence.

So for my friend, saying the words "thank you" sounded rude and cold. She felt like she was paying up for every favor and kindness, so she would not have to accept any *on* from her new American friends. In Japan they say that staying for a single night under someone else's roof creates a whole lifetime of on. Then, of course, on accumulates into giri, and all giri aspires to *ninjyō*, the most important emotion that any human being can ever experience. It is the feeling of secure, permanent connection with all other human beings; the Japanese simply define ninjyō as "human feeling." Thus, the graceful receipt of kindness is the glue that binds all human beings everywhere. Saying thank you cuts ninjyō off at the pass and makes it more difficult to experience genuine connection with other people.

THE SUMANAI SOCIETY

Over the years I have made it a point to educate all of my long-term psychotherapy clients and quite a few of my students about the difference between saying "thank you" and saying "Sumanai!" If we have grown close to and developed a strong relationship with someone, we don't want to say thank you (and good-bye). We want to say "It is not finished!" In other words, there will be more, and this relationship will grow into the future. It's a kind of shared relationship karma. This is a very simple idea that can play an important role in helping you come to terms with the harm that your anger does to your most important and intimate relationships.

So I conclude this chapter with an invitation for you to start your own Sumanai! society. Try to populate it with as much obligation (on) as you can muster, in the hope that it will eventually coalesce into giri and fill your heart with ninjyō. To get started on this project you need to complete two tasks, based on exercises adapted from Gregg Krech (2002).

A CONCLUDING MEDITATION: MINDFUL OBLIGATION

Make a list of the ten most important people in your life (excluding your spouse or partner), and then write down the three most important things that each has done for you. Search for some tangible way of directly communicating with each of those ten people and letting them know that these kindnesses are still in your memory, and that you are still very much connected with them because of the lasting memory of these acts and what they meant to you. If you choose to write or call them with this expression of your Sumanai, they will probably think you are a little odd, but I guarantee that you will make their day—maybe even their whole week!

Now you are ready to meditate on something even more central in your life. Think mindfully about, and preferably write down, everything that your spouse or partner does for you over the next couple of days. Reflect on every single loving, caring, kind, and attentive act that you receive from this wonderful person. Show that list to your partner, and express your deep appreciation for taking such wonderful care of you.

This is, indeed, the Buddha's path.

7

The Challenge
of Forgiveness

My computer recently had a psychotic episode. Approximately every ten minutes it would stop whatever it was doing and literally try to sell me something. I thought I could learn to work around the problem—dividing my computer time into discrete ten-minute chunks—but that didn't work. It was driving me crazy. Finally I realized I was powerless and I asked Pat, one of my students, for help. Pat downloaded some fancy software, which immediately isolated and destroyed a very nasty virus that I had inadvertently picked up while using the Internet. There was no possible way I could have completed this book (or anything else) while that virus had control over my computer's free will. Sometimes you just have to root out the alien demons in your hard drive in order to get on with your life.

THE DEMON IN YOUR HARD DRIVE

People do unspeakably cruel things to other human beings all the time. From a psychological perspective the truly remarkable thing is how resilient humans are even in the face of barbaric cruelty and extra-ordinary suffering. Most of the time, even after the worst experiences, we pick ourselves up, dust ourselves off, and go on to do what needs to be done. *But we never forget.*

In fact, it appears that we may be neurologically incapable of forgetting trauma. The evolutionary advantage of remembering the events surrounding extreme danger makes it so we can barely remember our last birthday party but we can immediately access clear and vivid memories of particular cruelties we have experienced. These memories are stored in our brains in an amazingly complicated way. We store verbal memories of bad events, but we also store visual memories, scent memories, taste memories, and even auditory memories. The memories, moreover, are among the most durable fixtures in our brains. Abused children retain detailed memories of their trauma for years after the abuse has stopped.

The effects of trauma often make the task of coping with even the normal stresses and strains of human life particularly difficult. People with trauma and abuse histories may find it extremely difficult to get their most important needs met in routine interactions with spouses and friends. This is because trauma, especially trauma in childhood, can effect significant structural changes in the very core of one's personality. Here is what one psychopathology textbook (Halgin and Whitbourne 2005) says about this process:

> Children who are raised in relatively healthy and responsive environments develop fundamental assumptions about the world as a benevolent and meaningful place and about themselves as worthy individuals. Because a traumatic event cannot be easily integrated with a positive view of oneself and the environment, or with a belief in the predictability and meaning of life events, a traumatic experience can lead to a shattering of those basic beliefs about the self and the world. For trauma victims, the world is no longer safe, predictable, and understandable; their sense of self may be jeopardized as they attempt to understand how they came to be the victims of horrible events or others' malevolent actions. It is no surprise, therefore, that the experience of trauma

can touch the deepest level of personality functioning and result in effects that last a lifetime. (182)

Post-Traumatic Stress Disorder (PTSD)

Post-traumatic stress disorder (PTSD) is the name given to the complex syndrome of psychological disturbance that affects at least 8 percent of the American population (Halgin and Whitbourne 2005). The symptoms of PTSD are involuntary and are generally triggered by environmental events that in some way mimic stimuli that were present during the original trauma.

The diagnosis of PTSD, which must be confirmed by a trained mental health professional, involves the analysis of an extensive psychological history as well as confirmation of a number of highly specific characteristic signs of the disorder. Generally speaking, the person with PTSD demonstrates symptoms of intrusion and avoidance (including intrusive thoughts, recurrent dreams, flashbacks, and avoidance of thoughts that are reminders of the trauma) and hyperarousal and numbing (including detachment, loss of interest, sleep disturbance, and emotional numbing) (Halgin and Whitbourne 2005).

For our purposes, PTSD is important because it is associated with hypervigilance, difficulty concentrating, significant levels of irritability, and frequent outbursts of anger. When anger is present in a person's life because of PTSD, it is essential that the person seek competent psychological counseling as soon as possible. If you are a veteran of military combat, have experienced a natural disaster, or have been the victim of or witnessed a violent crime, ask yourself whether your anger may be a small part of a much larger problem. If so, make an appointment with a mental health professional who has experience diagnosing and working with men with PTSD.

Intermittent Explosive Disorder

There are other ways your hard drive could have become infected with anger. One of these ways is intermittent explosive disorder, a rare psychological syndrome in which people demonstrate the following characteristics:

- Numerous episodes of "unresistable" aggressive impulses resulting in serious acts of assault or property destruction

- Angry episodes in which the level of aggressiveness is grossly out of proportion to the triggering event (Halgin and Whitbourne 2005)

The behavior described above is, of course, what you see in the road-rage guy, the guy who becomes wildly angry at sporting events, the spouse abuser, and the guy who can't hold a job because his behavior frightens the other employees. People who demonstrate intermittent explosive disorder virtually always have some other mental health problem as well. The usual comorbid disorders are substance abuse, depression, and obsessive-compulsive disorders. Treatments for this disorder frequently require hospitalization and psychotropic medication.

Sexual Abuse

At least half of the men I have treated for serious anger issues have reported some form of sexual victimization in their past. You know whether or not you are one of those men. The rest of the chapter should offer you a lot of things to think about if you have experienced sexual abuse, but there are a few points that need to be made that are specific to the anger in men who have been sexually abused.

First, you don't have to forgive, forget, or deny the abuse you have experienced. You don't have to "get over it" in order to stop being angry. The enduring anger stemming from a history of abuse remains forever in the unconscious mind, an arena that the psychoanalyst and prominent Buddhist thinker Mark Epstein (1995) calls the Realm of the Hungry Ghosts. Epstein uses this term to suggest how old, painful memories can come to dominate our current emotional lives in a powerful way—memories of trauma seem to want to devour our well-being, and it seems like they can never be satisfied.

As hungry as your own ghosts may seem to be, it is not necessary to compromise with evil in order to recover from its effects. It may be extremely helpful for you to join a support group for men who have had similar experiences. It may also be valuable to work with a therapist on a weekly or monthly basis until you can deal with what happened to you, so that you can understand and integrate your painful memories without poisoning your future with rage and hatred.

Second, the real problem is probably not the sexual activity that took place. It's pretty clear that children can be as sexual as opportunity permits them to be without experiencing any negative effects at all. The real problem is with the *shame* you're experiencing now because of the events that happened back then. Shame is a very important issue for men, and many men require years of support before they can come to terms with their shame over a huge variety of misdeeds. But focusing on the person and actions of the abuser does not speak to the issue of male shame. I believe that all men experience at least some legacy of shame; and the knowledge of that can provide a sort of common bond among men. Shame is the taproot of depression in men, and we spend a lot of our lives struggling with memories of being shamed. When shame becomes very strong we even experience shame about our shame. Shame deserves to be the object of its own mindful meditation. It is important for you to try as hard as you can not to cover up your shame with mindless anger.

Third, sexual abuse leaves a legacy of violation, dishonor, and distrust. If you were sexually victimized by a priest, a coach, a teacher, a scout leader, or any other person you genuinely looked up to, the thing that will stay with you for the rest of your life is the lie that took root in the heart of that relationship. I don't know whether anyone has ever been able to completely forgive another person for that sort of lie, but I do know that the legacy of that sort of betrayal is often an inability to ever fully trust another person again. Since the people who love you now were not the people who betrayed you then, they are going to be confused and hurt by your insistence on keeping up self-protective barriers. For their sake, and for your own, of course, you'll really want to work on that.

THE TAO OF FORGIVENESS

Forgiveness is a challenge for all of us, and a key component of your anger control program. Let's begin by talking about what forgiveness is, and later we'll look at what it is not.

What Is Forgiveness?

Experts don't seem to have come to any consensus about the nature of forgiveness, except for the widespread agreement that it is incredibly important—and exceptionally difficult to achieve. One interesting aspect of forgiveness is that it requires a substantial amount of power.

The power to forgive is associated with the authority of God, royalty, the state, and parents. I have never heard of a ritual of forgiveness in which the congregation forgives God for sending a plague or a convicted man forgives the king for throwing him in jail. The state can pardon a criminal, but the criminal doesn't forgive the state for not teaching him any marketable job skills, and your kids are unlikely to forgive you for acting like a real jerk last week.

So, this is an interesting place to open our inquiry into the nature of forgiveness. What does it take for you to be able to experience forgiveness, and for you to be able to serve it up?

Journal Exercise 7-1:
Receiving and Bestowing Forgiveness

Your assignment is first to reflect on an experience you have had of being forgiven. In your journal, write about the wrong that you had committed, who forgave you, how they forgave you, and what the consequence was of that act of forgiveness. Did the forgiveness truly signify the end of that person's anger toward you for the bad thing you did? How much time went by after the act of forgiveness before things were back to normal in your relationship?

Second, reflect on a time when you genuinely forgave a person for a wrong he or she had done to you. This time, record what this person had done, when and how you forgave him or her, and what the person's reaction was to being forgiven. Now, the really important questions: What happened to your anger after you granted the forgiveness? How long did it take to go away completely—if it ever did?

Third, examine the power balance between you and the other person in the first example, and then in the second example. What can you learn from this? Record your observations in your journal.

Prerequisites for Forgiveness

It is probably hard to know precisely why the person in the first example decided to forgive you, but can you figure out why *you* decided to forgive in the second example? It may have been because anger is just such a heavy load of rocks to have to carry around on your head. It may also have been because you were smart enough to realize that the only thing that anger ever creates is fear, anxiety, resentment, and ultimately, of course, more anger. As the Buddha once taught, it is impossible for hatred to be appeased by more hatred, and maybe we are conscious enough (most of the time) to realize that.

SELF-AWARENESS

The greatest two prerequisites for forgiveness, I suspect, are self-awareness and transcendent love. Most of the really angry people I have contact with strike me as having almost no self-awareness. They walk around in the world causing pain and inflicting trouble, and they appear to have absolutely no awareness of what they are doing. One of the angriest people I know can bring any conversation to a complete stop, just by entering the room. She has no idea that thirty seconds before she joins a conversation everyone is usually having a perfectly good time, and that her menacing presence of overwhelming negativity makes everyone scuttle for their protective hole in the sand.

Thus, the Buddhist writer Bhante Gunaratana (2002) teaches that any genuine forgiveness requires an aggrieved person to be 100 percent honest with himself. Does he really feel ready to let go of the hurt and give up that feeling of moral superiority? Forgiveness half given or insincerely offered is just an illusion, and not really forgiveness at all. Other writers (Hayes, Strosahl, and Wilson 1999) take this one step further and assert that forgiveness requires a person to be able to be at peace with him- or herself in order to be able to make the active choice to let the incident go.

Ron and Patricia Potter-Efron (1995) build on this theme of honesty and clarity about the self, counseling that forgiveness requires actively and knowingly giving up all claims against your enemies. Forgiveness, as they say in their book, is the ultimate act of free will, a clear and conscious choice in which you give up the right to (1) experience lingering resentments and (2) retain the option to make the person pay a little more some time later. The act of forgiving, they state, means completely putting the incident behind you, forgoing any later opportunity to right the scales of justice.

Robert Thurman's (2005) discussion of the nature of forgiveness doesn't describe forgiveness as a gracious act and a transcendent gift between human beings, as many Christian writers have done. As a Buddhist, Thurman is primarily concerned with the cleansing of his own heart and spirit, and with making sure that his conduct shines a bright light in the world. He hopes that his example will inspire others to live a more responsible and responsive life, but his argument with anger is that it poisons his soul and destroys his ability to live harmoniously in the world.

NECESSARY VIRTUES

Like Marvin Levine (2000), Robert Thurman wants us to see forgiveness as a reflection of the constant effort of a human being to follow the path of the Buddha. Forgiveness is an intentional human act that reflects one's strength of character; it occupies the same place in a person's well-ordered life as several other virtues:

- Tolerance

- Patience

- Forbearance

- Endurance

- Transcendent love

Thurman, in the spirit of the Dalai Lama, adds that "Our enemy is just our opportunity to practice this most rare and important transcendent virtue" (2005, 115). Anger stirs up enormous energies and vitality within us. One must seize this opportunity, and convert that energy and vitality into the service of *wisdom* that will deepen our practice of patience, forbearance, endurance, tolerance, and love. That is why, as we saw earlier, when he was asked why he was not full of hatred at the Chinese who had invaded his country, killed his people, and sent him into exile, the Dalai Lama replied, "They have stolen my country; but I will not let them steal my heart." But if you are going to effect that transformation, you must accept that the process will require sincere and deliberate Right Effort (Bankart 2003), and against considerable odds.

Journal Exercise 7-2:
Giving Thanks When It Is Least Expected

In chapter 6 I told you the story about Joel's success at taming his bratty sister with unexpected love. In exercise 6-2 I suggested that you surprise one of the angrier people you know with a small, unexpected gift. Now we'll carry this principle of loving kindness to a higher level. I have adapted this exercise from one developed for Jon Kabat-Zinn's (1994) stress-reduction program.

The next time someone angers you, gently place one hand over the middle of your chest, and place your other hand gently on top of that one. As you are interacting with this person who is trying to anger you, look him or her in the eye, smile, and, either silently or aloud, say the words, "Thank you; you have been my teacher." Write about your experience with this exercise in your journal.

You will discover, by the way, that if you place your hands over each other in the middle of your chest whenever you begin to feel anger being provoked, you will immediately have significantly more control over your emotional experience.

TRANSCENDENT LOVE

I think people in the Christian tradition spend more time talking about transcendent love than do people in the Buddhist tradition. Love is certainly another component of forgiveness. But I have found, as a lapsed Christian, that the message of Christian love is pretty complicated. Some time ago, a series of billboards were erected in my town by a local church that proclaimed, together with a wide range of graphic images, "Love Jesus or Go to Hell."

I'd never thought of Jesus as a dysfunctional parent before, but for the members of this particular church this was, evidently, the central message of the gospels. As a psychologist I guess I could say something like "Love Your Enemy—or Die of Cardiovascular Disease," but that somehow doesn't pack the same dramatic punch as a threat to send you to hell.

Nevertheless, transcendent love as the ultimate cure for anger is central to the message of all major religions, and it certainly was the message I took from my early religious training as a Christian. The

Buddha himself once said that anger is only appeased by love, but unfortunately he didn't really give any instructions about how to achieve that love when everything around you seems to be conspiring against it.

Yet, if you think deeply about forgiveness, you will probably discover that the only people you can really forgive are the people you truly love. You forgive your son for smashing up the car, your daughter for breaking your heart, your partner for being less than perfect when you really need someone who is perfect. I think it is a common understanding in our world that love and hate have far more in common with each other than they have with indifference and disregard.

In the following exercise we'll meditate on the relationship between love and hate, and we'll inquire what happens when love turns to hate.

Journal Exercise 7-3: Meditation on Love and Hate

Think of a person you despise, to the point of hating him or her. You'll want to choose someone actively involved in your life, not some mass murderer or a politician with views different from your own.

Take a few minutes and meditate on the depth of the revulsion you feel for that person. Ask yourself what it would take for you to give a kidney to this person if he or she were going to die without it. What would it take for you to forgive all of the horrible, miserable, and rotten things that person has done to you and others? Can you imagine ever being able to love him or her in the way that Jesus commanded, or the way the Buddha prescribed? What does it cost you to refuse to forgive this person? How heavy are the rocks in the box of hate that you carry on your head?

If you could dilute your anger at this person with a compassionate understanding of the pain he or she lives with, *how would your own life improve?*

What Forgiveness Is Not

Forgiveness may be a little easier to contemplate if we understand what is *not* part of forgiving someone.

FORGIVENESS IS NOT CHANGING YOUR MIND

Among the men I work with, much of their resistance to forgiveness is rooted in *principle*. A real man sticks by his principles, and he doesn't give in on what is right and important just for the sake of patching up real differences. These men believe that people who change their mind about important issues demonstrate weakness of character; they aren't fully to be trusted.

If you think about this for more than thirty seconds, though, it doesn't make any sense. What happens when the parents of a murdered child tell the court that they have chosen to forgive their child's murderer. Clearly they are not saying that they have changed their mind about wanting their child to be alive. What about the man who is angry at his daughter because she had an abortion? Can he sincerely forgive her, and still think that abortion is a terrible sin and an abomination? If a man is swindled by his longtime business partner in a shady transaction, can he forgive his partner without adopting or endorsing his partner's rotten business ethics?

For some reason these issues come up quite often in situations that involve sexual behavior. I know dozens, if not hundreds, of young men whose fathers—and sometimes mothers—won't "forgive" them for being gay. How does a son make sense of this? How could his own father hate him for something that he simply *is*? The son believes that his father loves him, but he also believes that his father hates him. Does it make any sense for a father to "forgive" his son for being wired differently? Yet fathers will tell me that they can't replace their anger and rage with love and compassion because the *moral principle* is more important than the relationship between these two human beings.

FORGIVENESS IS NOT DENIAL

When I counsel men who have been the victims of abuse, neglect, and parental rejection, we almost always run up against the problem that the *idea* of forgiveness seems to feel like *denial* that anything bad ever happened. It feels as if forgiving the man who molested you when you were a teenager is the same as giving in to the lies and deceits that that man fed you in order to get what he wanted from you.

This problem is often complicated by the fact that the denial is an ongoing process for one or both parties to the offense. Can you forgive someone who abused you but is still in denial about it? Probably not, unless you are exceptionally Christlike or have studied with the Dalai Lama for the past thirty years.

But this raises a number of really important questions.

Who does the forgiveness really benefit? The person who is learning how to unload the rocks from the box on his head is the one who benefits the most from the act of forgiveness. Maybe it lets the wrongdoer escape from a bit of censure, but I bet it isn't nearly as much as you might think.

Who is going to start the process of de-escalating the problem between you two? This is an important issue in Buddhism, and possibly in Christianity as well. Back in the days when I counseled couples, I always preached that the partner who *won* any particular fight was the partner who most gracefully *ended* it. Maybe your father's denial about his cruelty to you when you were a boy can't begin to fall apart until you approach his heart with compassionate forgiveness.

Do you need this struggle in order to stay focused and sane? Many years ago my son borrowed his mother's first-generation, stainless-steel Walkman, which we had bought in Japan. Then, like an idiot, he traded it to a pal for some worthless junk. My task in the family is to keep this story alive to make sure that mother and son don't gang up on me. Of course, this is all a family joke now, but it's not a joke that a great many people can't let go and forgive. They may have this difficulty not so much because the other party is in denial, but because it allows them to keep the upper hand in their dealings with that person.

Can you let go of the hope of vengeance—the desire that someday you will be able to prove that that person is, has been, and always will be wrong? This is really the problem of *attachment* writ large. If you are so attached to the idea that this person is *wrong*, it seems almost unnatural to just let the moral trophy of your righteousness go to the recycling center. True reconciliation between you is not likely to happen as long as you are unwilling to forgo the rewards of your moral superiority.

Would you even know what you need to hear in order to put a stop to all this nonsense? How often have you been in a situation where you hear yourself saying, for the fiftieth time, "Hey, I'm sorry! It was my fault.

I'm really, really, really sorry. I'll do my best to make sure it will never happen again!" But either you aren't saying it right, or you've made the speech too many times before, or the person just isn't ready yet to let it go.

The point of these questions is simple. To achieve emotional peace, you will need to grant forgiveness to those who have done you harm. This does not mean turning your back on the truth of what happened in the past, but opening a door to the future. The other person may or may not ever recognize the harm he or she has done you, but you will at the least stop poisoning your own heart with the desire for revenge.

FORGIVENESS IS NOT FORGETTING

In my work with boys and men who have been victimized, I find that many men fear that if they forgive their enemy they will be just setting themselves up to be victimized all over again. I believe that people are sincere in this belief, but I also sincerely believe that their fear is almost completely groundless.

There's a folk expression in the Midwest that goes, "Fool me once, shame on you. Fool me twice, shame on me." I went through a period in my life when my son was away at college when I seemed to be consistently trying to destroy our relationship. Every single time he drove home to visit us in his old rust bucket of a car, he would park as far away from the garage doors as he possibly could. Not twice or even three times but seven or eight times, I backed out of my garage without looking, right into his car. By the time the kid was a sophomore his right front door was more Bondo than it was Toyota. So "shame on him" for assuming his father would remember to look behind him when he backed out of the garage? Or "shame on me" for being so completely mindless when I put my car in reverse?

We solved the problem when my wife insisted that I give up my garage space to Charlie. This allowed me to suffer the painful anxiety that he would back out of the garage without looking, and do the same to *my* passenger-side door. This little technique definitely made me more mindful, and now it is my wife who fairly routinely wrecks our cars.

It is a fact of nature that forgiveness does not lead to forgetting. I think I would argue that forgiveness, far from making us less mindful, actually increases our awareness of the world around us. If you can forgive that crooked business partner or that unfaithful lover, it doesn't make you oblivious. Instead, it makes you more realistic—less paranoid, and more perceptive. If forgiveness makes you wiser, and I believe it does, then forgiveness makes you less likely to fall into the same pattern of mistakes, misjudgments, and false assumptions the next time around. And no matter whether that statement is 100 percent true or not, I see no evidence whatsoever showing that people who have forgiven (or the people who have been forgiven) also forget what they have experienced, a point made with great elegance by Mark Epstein in his book *Going on Being* (2001).

FORGIVENESS IS NOT UNFAIR

The person who has been forgiven does not *get away* with something. It is true that he or she has received a *gift*, one that may or may not be deserved, but there is nothing unfair or unwise about your decision to give that gift.

If you only had thirteen units of forgiveness to give out over the span of your entire life, how would you decide who "deserved" them? Would you save them all for your dad, who accidentally (albeit repeatedly) damaged your crappy old car—or would you save them for the ones who deliberately and knowingly betrayed your love, abused your trust, and trivialized your friendship?

Thank God we don't have to answer that question. There is no limit to the amount of forgiveness every human being can dish out in this lifetime. And the person who keeps receiving forgiveness because he or she keeps messing up over and over again? Maybe that person is the one who most desperately needs a small mountain of forgiveness in order to get his or her life back on track.

What would be *fair* is if every person got pretty much what they need and if we paid it out according to the quality and quantity of our own treasure. The treasure behind this forgiveness is equanimity, peace, genuine well-being, and compassion for all living things.

Robert Frost (1949, 53) once wrote, "Home is the place where, when you have to go there/They have to take you in." But in this poem the speaker's wife disagrees. She says, "I should have called it/ Something you somehow haven't to deserve." The next exercise is a meditation on the question of what you *deserve* in the way of loving kindness and forgiveness.

Journal Exercise 7-4:
Getting What You Deserve

In your journal, start by making a list of two or three people who have freely given you forgiveness in your life. Just write down their names, and a few notes about what you remember receiving from them.

Now reflect on the wrong you did that led to that forgiveness and compassion. Did you really *deserve* all that consideration you received?

Now think of two or three people who may or may not *deserve* your forgiveness, but whose lives clearly reflect the need for it. Are you willing to be that generous with them?

Mindfully meditate on this question for a little while, and then write what you will do to resolve this contradiction between what you have received in the form of forgiveness, and what you have chosen to freely and openly give.

SELF-FORGIVENESS: A FINAL MEDITATION

The solemn fact is that the demon in your hard drive is looking at you in the mirror. The person who most desperately needs your forgiveness is you. And I suspect you already knew that, but there is a huge problem: deep down, you don't believe that you *deserve* to be forgiven.

Giving up some forgiveness to someone who has messed you up is probably child's play compared with looking yourself square in the eye and giving yourself the same second chance.

All of the issues related to forgiveness are magnified ten or twenty times when you think about the complicated challenge of self-forgiveness. What I am asserting is that the deepest, most pervasive, and most corrosive anger you experience is always directed squarely at yourself, and you can't imagine how to turn that around.

If all this meditation, mindfulness, and rational therapy has any value whatsoever, its ultimate application has to be to yourself.

A Moral Accounting

So, it is time for you to engage in a serious moral accounting. Start by asking yourself the following questions:

1. What can I remember having stolen?

2. What lies can I remember telling?

3. What people have I harmed?

4. In what ways have I been most wrong in my bullheaded life?

You have lied. You have stolen. You have acted like a creep. You have broken your word; you have failed as a friend, a lover, and probably a father. You have, from time to time, been a world-class asshole, and you have rarely admitted it.

Guess what—so have I. So has your dad. So has everyone you know or ever have known. We are *all* fallible, fucked-up human beings, and, although we probably don't deserve them, we all need second, third, fourth, and ninety-ninth chances to make it right. *We are all fallible, fucked-up human beings, just like everyone else.*

In Buddhism you would be encouraged at this point to put your list of wrongs in the back of your mind and go out to work physically, mentally, and spiritually to make the world a better place. Doing good things, thinking good thoughts, striving to leave the world a better place than you found it—these are all good and important things. They improve your karma, they reduce the size of the writing on the list that you just stuck in your head. What was it Jesus said? "Go forth, and sin no more."

A CONCLUDING MEDITATION: A SALVATION MANTRA

To put you on the road to self-forgiveness, and to encourage you to go forth, sin no more, and make the world a better place for everyone else,

I've designed a *mantra* for you. A mantra is just a pattern of sounds, words, or phrases that you repeat over and over in your head to keep your attention firmly locked on reality. Here is your self-forgiveness mantra. Start repeating.

> *I am a human being. Just like all other human beings.*
> *I hope I am good enough; I want to be good enough;*
>   *I am good enough.*
> *I deserve to treat myself as well as I treat all others.*
> *I am a human being; I am being human.*
> *I am a human, being.*

8

Provoking the Dragon

You have covered all the basic steps in this book's anger control program, and you now know, intellectually at least, just about as much as I do about mindfulness, Buddhism, and using a systematic, mindful, incremental plan to become, and to be, a less angry human being. In this chapter we will put what you have learned to the test.

The challenge in teaching folks about anger management is not coming up with proven ways to help them control their anger. Controlled studies (Deffenbacher, Oetting, and DiGiuseppe 2002; Del Vecchio and O'Leary 2004; DiGiuseppe and Tafrate 2001, 2003) show that just about every anger management program under the sun can be effective in reducing felt and expressed anger in people who complete the program. Following the program outlined in this book will quite effectively guide you toward becoming a less angry guy, and it will set your life moving in a very positive direction. That's a promise.

So what's the catch? Every single anger management program used in contemporary psychotherapy and counseling, including this one, has to be practiced on a regular basis or its effectiveness will begin to decline and then eventually disappear. So you have to practice, practice, practice if you want this investment to pay off for you.

But there's an even bigger catch just over the horizon. You have to practice in real time, and without avoidance. In fact, to make this program really pay off, you really have to go out there and track down some people and situations that are destined to challenge your ability to control your anger to its very limits. And you have to do that fairly regularly.

That's why the title of this chapter is "Provoking the Dragon."

A CAUTIONARY TALE ABOUT SOCIALISM

There's an old story about a Maine farmer named Fred who went down to Boston to listen to a talk by Norman Thomas on the glories of socialism. Fred came back to his village all fired up by what he had heard, and he began to spread the word about socialism among his fellow farmers. One day, as Fred was talking socialism, his friend Silas interrupted him, asking, "You mean to tell me, Fred, that under socialism if you had two barns, you'd share that second one with me?"

"Yes, Silas, I do," replied the farmer. "And if I had two pigs, I'd share one of them with you, and if I had two hay rigs, I'd share one of them, too."

Silas scratched his chin, and then he asked, "So, Fred, if you had two cows, let's say, under socialism, you'd share one of them with me?"

The farmer stamped his foot and said, "Damn it, Silas, you *know* I've got two cows."

Fred's enthusiasm about socialism was theoretical; he really didn't consider that it meant he'd have to share his cows. Similarly, you can be pretty enthusiastic over your anger control program, but that won't really mean very much until you put it to the test in the real world.

A CAUTIONARY TALE ABOUT ANGER MANAGEMENT

Until you feel completely confident that your anger control strategies are all in place and working smoothly, you will need to pay close attention to the situations in your life that are apt to trigger a strong negative emotional response in you. You'll find a list of a dirty dozen of the most common triggers below, but please be aware that you probably have triggers based on your own personal history that you will need to add to this list. On the other hand, some of the dirty dozen may not trouble you very much, so you can drop them from your list.

Journal Exercise 8-1: A Dirty Dozen Anger Triggers

Complete this exercise by recording how you respond to each of the following common anger triggers in daily life. In your journal, write your observations about how you handle (or don't) each of the triggers described below.

1. Perceived disrespect

    - Does this seem worse when it comes from someone above you or below you in social rank?

    - Is it worse coming from a man or from a woman?

    - What kind of disrespect is most disturbing to you?

2. A challenge to your authority

    - In what kinds of situations is this most likely to occur?

    - What form does the challenge take?

    - What are the motives of the person who is challenging you?

3. Embarrassment

    - Do you get angry when something happens that makes you look or feel foolish?

    - Does your sense of humor fail you?

4. Feeling overloaded with work or personal problems

    - Some men experience anger when they are feeling sad; what might you feel before an anger episode?

5. Expectations set too high

6. Experiencing harm or personal injury because of another person

   ■ Is the harm intentional or accidental?

7. A racial, ethnic, or sexual insult or slur

8. Being interrupted while speaking, or doing something important

9. Finding yourself in a situation where you had difficulty in the past

10. Being told what to do by a person who is not in authority to do so, or being told to do something rather than being asked nicely

11. Someone not doing what you asked them to do

12. Excessive drinking

Early Warning Signs

When you encounter one of these triggers you need to immediately shift your attention away from the source of the trigger, and take a brief time-out to check your current state of well-being. You might even want to complete a quick body scan, invoke your personal relaxation image, or repeat a mantra to yourself.

The importance of paying attention to the early warning signs of an angry episode is to give yourself a heads-up that will allow you to reorient yourself toward self-control and away from following in your old destructive path. The goal is for you to plug in rather quickly to a problem-solving, emotionally stable way of dealing with the problem in front of you.

HIGH-RISK SETTINGS

You will want to pay attention to where you are and what you are doing when you encounter your dragon. Is it pretty specific to certain settings at work, or when you are playing softball, or when you are trying to straighten out your kids? Being more aware of high-risk settings allows you to enter those situations with a plan to remain calm, rational, and on top of your game.

HIGH-RISK FEELINGS

Certain situations can put you at risk, but so can certain feelings. You may discover, for example, that sexual frustration puts you on edge and makes you kind of grouchy. And, as I've already mentioned, there may be certain mood states, like depression, anxiety, frustration, and boredom, that put you at risk of becoming angry. Awareness of these mood and feeling states will present you with an opportunity to change what you are doing, so you make things more comfortable and agreeable for yourself.

AVOIDING ESCALATION

Remember the idea that the person who successfully ends an argument is really the person who has won the argument? This idea leads to a larger point: you have to know when to *exit the field.*

If you are arguing about politics or baseball or who makes the best burgers in town, it's probably a dumb conversation anyway, and *it doesn't really matter who wins or loses.* You may discover that your worst anger episodes happen in really dumb situations, and that anyone who is sane and rational would recognize that the best thing to do would be to just shut up and let go of the darned rope!

The Japanese have an old saying about how to avoid domestic problems between husbands and wives: *Otokowa damatte biru.* This translates roughly to "Men should keep silent and drink beer."

Maybe drinking beer isn't a good idea for you; but chances are that you have more than a few opportunities in your life to keep silent and just let yourself observe the scene from the throne of your superior wisdom. Try to take pride in the number of arguments that you avoid, end, and concede, because every one of these arguments could otherwise put you in hot water emotionally. As a wise man once said, "Generally speaking it is better to keep your mouth shut and have people suppose you a fool than it is to open your mouth and confirm it."

Cognitive Events in Anger Escalation

There may have been times in your life when you were just itching for a fight or an argument, and you knew exactly where to find it and how to start it. I certainly hope those days are behind you by now.

More often, you have probably found yourself becoming angry in situations where you weren't looking for any trouble but trouble somehow found you. Cognitive therapists have spent a lot of time studying what goes on inside a person's mind when this sort of thing happens, and the results of their research are important to understand. The most respected researcher in this field is the psychologist Albert Ellis, who has written literally dozens of great books on what is widely known as rational emotive behavior therapy. Below are some of Ellis's ideas.

THE FOUR STAGES OF THINKING YOURSELF INTO A CORNER

■ Stage one: *Awfulizing*. Something goes wrong, someone says the wrong thing, the world isn't the way you want it and need it to be. So you start thinking about this, and over the space of a few minutes, a few hours, or a few days you come to convince yourself that this thing is simply and tragically awful.

In this stage you decide that just about nothing worse could ever happen to a human being. It is terrible, tragic, unbelievable, and absolutely unacceptable. And it all happened to *you*!

■ Stage two: *Icantstandititis*. This is a terrible, nearly fatal psychiatric disease in which you come to realize that you simply can't tolerate what is happening for one more moment. Alcoholics and drug abusers are the reigning kings and queens of *Icantstandititis*. They have virtually zero tolerance of frustration, and they demand that every unpleasant, uncomfortable, disagreeable, and disturbing thing be removed from their presence, *this instant!* Ellis calls people with *icantstandititis* "BFBs," which stands for "big fucking babies." Ellis has wisely asked whether any committed BFB could ever reasonably hope to have genuine self-esteem.

Now that you have established that something absolutely terrible, horrible, and completely unbearable has happened to you, and you know that there is no way you can live with this horrible thing for even five more minutes, read on for the next phase of escalation.

■ Stage three: *Musterbation*. Once a person has achieved the anger and resentment necessary to become completely and absolutely self-righteous, he enters that stage of thinking that Ellis calls *musterbation*. Musterbation is a form of self-abuse characterized by strident claims that other people in the world *ought not*, *should not*, and *must not* treat them in this way. Can you hear yourself talking like this? Hard-core musterbators are great fun to travel with, aren't they? Doesn't it make your day to be waiting for a plane and hear three or four professional muster-bators telling the gate personnel that they *must* be in Denver by 3:00, and the airline had better make the snowstorm stop or, by God, they will call a supervisor!

The tyrant musterbator's demand to speak to a supervisor signals advancement to the fourth stage of cognitive anger escalation.

■ Stage four: *You Are All Damned for All Eternity to Burn Forever in Hell with No Hope of Mercy!* By the time that your anger has reached the fire-and-brimstone stage, all the other passengers are cheering for you to be thrown off the flight, and there are bets being made on whether you will be struck down by a stroke right there in the terminal or someone will just come along and slap you silly. By this point the anger has escalated into a serious emotional, physical, and cognitive event. The prefrontal portion of your brain has simply shut down, and you have about the same grace, wisdom, and dignity as a three-year-old who desperately needs a time-out in the corner.

IN PRAISE OF A LITTLE STOICISM

A common theme appears in a lot of writing about "what's wrong with men today" in the popular media. Men, we are told, need to learn how to become more emotionally expressive, especially when we are in the presence of our partners. The interesting thing about this advice is that it is based on the assumption that emotional expressiveness is an unqualified good thing. Men (and boys, of course) should become more open about crying, expressing joy, and letting disappointment show. Maybe this is good advice, but you have to wonder if the writers who say these things also think that men should be more expressive about their anger! Most likely, they don't think that anger is the sort of manly feeling that men should be encouraged to express.

Are men too stoic? Should we be encouraging boys to cry in school, and our colleagues at work to share more of their emotional lives with us? Perhaps, but I believe that masculine stoicism may be a bit underrated as a virtue. Consider the following.

A man was once driving down a rural interstate highway, hauling his horse in a trailer behind his truck. Without warning, the car that was in the process of passing him pulled over suddenly right in front of his bumper and sharply braked—evidently because the driver suddenly noticed a state police car parked in the median.

The man hit his brakes and tried to maneuver his truck and trailer into the passing lane. The horse trailer turned over on the median and a second later the truck flipped on its side and skidded to a stop just a few feet from the oncoming traffic.

The man was in great pain and trapped in the debris of the truck cab; he began calling loudly for help. His horse, which had been thrown from the trailer onto the median, was howling in pain and struggling to get to its feet on its broken legs. Hurrying over to the accident scene, the state trooper passed right by the moaning man to where the horse was thrashing on the grass next to the smashed trailer. A second later a single shot rang out, and the horse became silent. The officer, gun in hand, came over to the truck with his gun still in his hand, looked inside the truck, and asked, "And how are *you* feeling?"

Sometimes a little stoicism can be a good thing; sometimes being overly "expressive" can be a bad strategy. Albert Ellis tells people that he developed the principles of rational emotive behavior therapy after reading the writings of the ancient Greek-Roman stoic philosopher Epictetus, who argued that a man's duty is to fulfill his own needs and responsibilities as a sociable human being, but also to accept his fate without complaint. He argued that anger was almost entirely a matter of habit, and as such one must control one's emotions in order to do nothing which may tend to increase it. He added: "If you would cure anger, do not feed it. Say to yourself: 'I used to be angry every day; then every other day; now only every third or fourth day.' When you reach thirty days offer a sacrifice of thanksgiving to the gods."

So while perhaps you would be well advised to be more emotionally available and expressive in your daily life, it may also, from time to time, be quite a good thing to have the ability to "suck it up, and move on" so that you do not unnecessarily feed the habit of your anger.

COMING DOWN

The hope, of course, is that by becoming mindfully aware of the ways in which particular situations cause you to feed your temper habit you will be able to shut the anger system down before you get even partway through the launch sequence.

Throughout this book you have encountered dozens of ideas and strategies for accomplishing this in the long term. When you are actually confronted by traffic gridlock, an overbooked flight, or a recalcitrant child, however, you'll need something that you can put into effect in seconds, not days or weeks. In the next section we'll look at a variety of cooling-off techniques that you can practice when you are not angry, so that they will be fully available to you when the need arises.

Short-Term Anger Management Strategies

The goal of all these strategies is twofold. First you want to clear your mind, so you can think straight. Then you want to be able to calm yourself down, so you can make sure that the episode does not escalate.

- *Take constructive action.* You need a plan, an actual thought-out strategy, for dealing with the situation. You need to get into problem-solving mode and start thinking like one of those exceptionally calm airport supervisors, not an irate customer. You've been in this kind of pickle before, so you know what the alternatives and options are. You need to make some phone calls, organize some alternative arrangements, find out whom you need to deal with, and use the unexpected free time to your advantage. David Reynolds's 1984 book *Constructive Living* offers dozens of ideas and strategies for developing the ability to approach problems from a helpful perspective.

- *Remove yourself from the front line.* As Colin Powell advised both George Bush and his son, never get yourself into a tight situation without having an *exit strategy*. If you are frustrated to the point of distraction, remove yourself physically from the situation. Go somewhere to cool off, collect your wits, and regroup. It is amazing how effective this is, and it is also amazing how few people do this once they get on a roll. An important aspect of this is to have your *exit lines* fully rehearsed. You don't impulsively storm away from the rental car counter shouting a curse at the clerk; you calmly thank the person who has been trying to help you and announce that you are going to give the competition a try.

- *Unpack your funny bone.* Laughter is a great defuser in all sorts of difficult situations. Take advantage of your natural ability to make other people laugh. Make sure you don't use humor to put the other person down, but instead try to lighten up the entire situation by looking at it as if it's a funny story that you'll be telling at the office next week.

- *Star in your own movie.* Think of yourself as a heroic character—the star of the movie about your life. You don't want to look like an idiot up there on the screen. You have to be cool, clever, handsome, self-assured, and amazingly admirable. You don't want to be cast as the crazy psycho who can't figure out how to solve his own problems.

- *Reduce your arousal level.* You know how to do a body scan. You have experience with relaxation. You might have even started to feel comfortable with mindfulness meditation and paying attention to your breath. Now is definitely *not* the time to slam a few beers or start thinking about how it is always *you* that the system chooses to mess on. Find someplace relatively quiet and semiprivate, and take a five-minute time-out to regulate your breathing, mop your face, straighten your tie. Be cool.

- *Treat yourself.* A few years ago I counseled a college student, Jack, who had had a very unpleasant run-in with a very aggressive bigot. The bigot told my client that he didn't want "his kind" around his dorm and tried to provoke my guy into a physical fight. Jack successfully walked away from the encounter without provoking the bigot, and he took pride in not losing his cool. I asked Jack what he did when the event was finished, and he replied, "I bought myself a really nice sweater."

- *Always be assertive.* Assertiveness is the skill of clearly and effectively communicating your needs and requirements. It means being able to explain what you want, and articulate what you think is fair, being neither aggressive nor wimpy or whiny about it. Assertiveness is really an attitude that a person takes in interactions with other people, especially in difficult situations. Assertiveness is extremely important in close relationships, because it requires you to acknowledge that you understand the other person's perspective but not back down from something that is important to you. If, for example, you and your partner argue about your sexual relationship, assertiveness requires you to acknowledge what your partner thinks and feels about it, but it also permits you to state as clearly as possible what you hope can change in that relationship. The same principle can be applied to arguments about money, disciplining the kids, interactions with relatives, or any other area of life where the rights and preferences of various people have to be put into some kind of balance.

- *Act with grace under fire.* Probably all of the above points could be subsumed under this idea. Ernest Hemingway wrote numerous short stories and novels about men who either demonstrated or failed to demonstrate grace under pressure; it was pretty much the virtue that Hemingway most admired and respected in a man. I can't tell you how to live your life with grace, but I can suggest that you think about the importance of grace, dignity, and "never letting them see you sweat." If you happen to be in a sexual, ethnic, or racial minority, or if you have a visible disability, living your public life with grace, honor, and dignity is probably the most important thing you can do to face down the bigots and the bullies out there—who live their lives without ever experiencing grace.

CONFRONTING THE DRAGON

In the first portion of this chapter I've been trying to prepare you for the realities you will likely encounter out in the real world, where your newfound anger management skills will be tested. It is important for you to take this advice seriously and anticipate challenges, because you don't want to be like the alcoholic who falls off the wagon of sobriety just because he eats a single rum ball. The world is full of people and situations just waiting for the opportunity to piss you off and watch you fail.

Relapse Prevention Training

Anticipating rough spots in the road ahead is what *relapse prevention training* is all about. Without thinking seriously about relapse prevention, you can't expect to stay on the course you want to be on. So below is a pretty good list of potential difficulties and warning signs, so you can make sure you are forearmed by being forewarned. Of course, don't try to avoid difficult people and situations. Expose yourself to them gradually and purposefully, if possible, and be well rehearsed in how to respond.

GOING IN OVER YOUR HEAD—ON PURPOSE

Having said that, I now encourage you to do just the opposite of the above advice. With the guidance of this book close at hand and your nearly complete journal fresh in your mind, I'd like to propose a sort of controlled burn to test out your firefighting equipment.

Journal Exercise 8-2: The Controlled Burn

There are some things in this world that are important not to compromise about. There are some situations where it is appropriate to be angry, and to express that anger. Race hatred may be one of those things. Pedophilia is another. Perhaps you feel that sending our kids off to die in Iraq is dead wrong, or perhaps you think that people who oppose the struggle for freedom in the Middle East are dead wrong. The key idea is to confront something that you think is monstrously wrong, evil, and nonnegotiable.

Your task is to hold this upsetting and unpleasant thought in your mind. Then examine your angry dragon when he roars out of his cave to take on truly awful things. You should engage in this anger-provoking meditation in order to become mindful about the changes that it brings about in the following:

- Your thought processes, especially your ability to think clearly

- Your biology, especially your muscle tension and blood pressure

- Your seriousness of purpose about this issue; the sincerity of your strong feelings

- Your ability to monitor and control these angry processes

Then record what you have learned in your journal.

BEING PASSIONATE AND BEING RESILIENT

Your dragon is passionate. Your dragon is righteous (but not self-righteous, I hope). Your dragon should never give up the struggle and never accept an evil that can be reformed, educated, or voted out of office. Your dragon must be willing to risk its freedom and even its life if necessary. You would not think twice about protecting your kids from evil or defending your country against some fanatical terrorist.

Which is all well and good. However, your dragon must also be resilient, smart, and self-aware. A dragon isn't much good if it isn't at least as confident of its effectiveness and power as it is of its moral integrity. In other words, your anger has to be grounded in optimism and hope as well as moral certainty and outrage. Of course, dragons are neither easy to come by nor inexpensive to maintain, so you also need to be practical and realistic.

FOUR UNCOMMON DRAGON VIRTUES

So here are four basic attributes that you must train your righteous-anger dragon to possess and to manifest when it is important enough for him to come out of his cave.

Empathy. If the dragon drops to the moral level of his enemies, then it doesn't matter whether or not he prevails, because he has already lost the struggle. The empathy behind your anger must cause you to constantly keep yourself and your anger in perspective. It requires a cool anger, not a hot temper. The diamond center of empathy is compassion; if you strike your enemy without compassion, then there is no goodness in your actions.

The operating principle behind empathy is, of course, the Golden Rule: always treat other people the way you want to be treated. If your victory over evil is only going to change who controls the keys to the prison of ignorance and cruelty, then you are blind to your original purpose. That, of course, is why revenge is never a wise or productive strategy in any moral struggle. Philosophers have suggested that the questions "What is it that I hope to accomplish?" and "Are my methods consistent with my larger goals?" are crucial in order to make sure you stay attuned to your true purpose in your struggle.

Self-monitoring. Your dragon must possess both self-awareness and awareness of what other people are seeing and thinking as you go about your mission. Not too long ago a story appeared in the news about a man who was arrested for shooting his car to death. He had gone out to his miserable-piece-of-junk vehicle and pumped two full magazines of heavy-duty ammunition into its rusting corpse. The arrest, of course, was for illegally discharging a firearm in a dangerous manner.

I confess to having stopped for a minute in sheer admiration of the audacity of the act. I too have owned cars that richly deserved this kind of an end. But my wife's reaction was wiser. "What kind of a nut case do you suppose he is?" she asked. And I had to concede that the words "nut case" probably summed it up pretty well.

The actions of the dragon must reflect the nobility of the cause. You really do have to ask yourself how the history of your act will be written. Was John Brown a heroic righteous crusader for the abolition of slavery and the end of human beings owning other human beings? Or was he a crazy psychopath who dragged his country into a brutal and devastating civil war? The truth is that while we may be able to empathize with the guy who murdered his vehicle, shooting your car will never raise you to the level of heroism in other people's eyes, by any definition of that term.

So you'll want to ask yourself the following questions:

- What words will sympathetic observers use to describe you?

- How would you like history to remember you?

- What would Jesus/the Buddha/Joan of Arc do in this situation?

- Are you likely to achieve what you want to accomplish, given the methods you have chosen?

- What are the most likely unintended consequences of your actions?

- Would it be okay for your children to watch you in this situation?

Knowing what you can control, and recognizing what you can't. We might add to this phrase "and being able consistently to exercise the wisdom to tell the difference." It's great that you have the *commitment* to make a positive difference in the world. It is admirable that you have stepped up to the *challenge* of making the world a better place. But do you have the wisdom to know what you can *control* and what you can't?

Of course, this, as you will know if you have raised teenagers, is largely a matter of teamwork, guesswork, and more than a little good luck. It is a struggle to know what can be subjected to our will, and what remains beyond our control. There is very little point in exercising your anger against forces of nature, high tides, and other people's sexuality.

To put this virtue into perspective, please consider adopting the following two really fundamental bottom-line rules:

1. Never enter a situation intending to act as a change agent until and unless you can identify at least three positive changes that you can clearly specify, that are doable, and that a good number of other people also want to see made.

2. Scratch off the list any of those items that will only happen if and when other people change in substantial and significant ways.

Always remaining connected to others. This is the principle of leadership. It is also the principles of charisma, persuasion, and inspiration. Probably the best way to inspire others to your cause is to be the kind of person that other people want to be like—or, more important, being the kind of person that other people want their kids to be like.

It's not enough to be trustworthy, brave, thrifty, cheerful, and friendly—offer other people a glimpse into a depth of character and integrity that will inspire them to join you in your crusade. You can accomplish this by establishing yourself as a generous and kind person, not just a hell-raiser with a thorn in his shorts. Demonstrate compassionate awareness of other people, not just your crusade against the evil that is your enemy.

A FINAL MINDFUL MEDITATION

Jon Kabat-Zinn asks a powerful and important question in his book *Wherever You Go There You Are* (1994, 207): "What is my job on this planet—with a capital J?" By way of clarification, Kabat-Zinn asks, "What do I care about so much that I would pay to do it?" He suggests that you think of the universe as your employer, regardless of what organization cuts your paycheck.

Journal Exercise 8-3: Your Job on This Planet

Your task is to meditate on the questions that Kabat-Zinn raises about your true mission in this life. Is it to fight injustice; raise happy, healthy, and productive kids; make more money than Bill Gates; create a little more love and peace than existed before you got here; or put the fear of God in every sinner?

Think about this question for a while, and in your journal make a list of the four or five most important contributions you could make to the well-being of the universe.

Does this mission, your Job on the planet, remind you about the most important reasons you want to stay alive?

Next, two more tasks. First, write a performance review of your mission so far. Should you give yourself a big merit raise? Or have you been slacking off? What can you start doing right now to show improvement on your next performance evaluation?

Second, if you never, ever again lost your temper, exercised your anger, or called forth your dragon, would you be more or less likely to accomplish your Job on this planet fully and effectively?

Take some time to reflect on your conclusions after completing this exercise.

Afterword: Waking Up Your Inner Buddha

The goal of this book has been to help you find a way to live your life as if it really mattered. Which, of course, means that you had to explore the possibility that *you* really matter. Despite the pressures of a culture that wants you to believe that you only matter to the degree that you have the right material stuff like money, power, and physical attractiveness, you matter primarily because you have a human heart. This is what we mean when we say that mindfulness meditation is a way to awaken the Buddha nature in everyone.

In the end, all that the practice of mindfulness is really concerned about is your heart. When you engage the world mindfully, you engage it with an open, aware, and nonjudgmental heart. Mindfulness encourages you to pay attention to the real depths of reality, and it is that attention that defines what it means to be a complete, awake, and fully functioning human being.

Because mindful awareness is by nature not only analytical and discerning but also holistic and exploratory, it is naturally oriented toward growth and wisdom. It moves us toward maturity and completion. It is naturally compassionate, but it is not phobic of pain and suffering, because it accepts responsibility for making the lives of all beings more sustainable.

That's why this book has been mostly about you, and less about your anger. As I stressed in the first chapter, you are not your anger. You never were. Anger contaminated your mind and your heart, and it is probably still a significant challenge to your well-being and your spiritual engagement with the world. But I hope, if you have learned nothing else in this book, you have learned that anger is not something that just happens to you but is instead a warning that your awareness has become clouded, distorted, and lacking in genuine awareness.

The bottom line is that the contaminating poison of anger has to be replaced with the power of loving kindness. In *Meeting the Monkey Halfway* (2000), Ajahn Sumand Bhikkhu, a Buddhist monk, advises us to direct loving kindness to our feelings, moods, and perceptions in order to eradicate anger from our hearts.

> Undercut the power of anger by seeing it in the present. Look intently into all its aspects and it will lose its power. Discard every layer of anger; look into your reactions in relation to the offender. Why are you angry? What do you wish to do with this anger? How far and in what direction do you want to go with it? How significant is this in your life? Is this anger worth jeopardizing your well-being? Is it worth all the time you are spending on it? The exercise of questioning your way through your anger will effectively force you into facing the realities of that moment. It will also give you the opportunity to answer those questions honestly. At the end of your investigation, you can be sure that you have lost the momentum of that anger and, therefore, have regained control over your otherwise runaway emotions. This is one of the great escapes from suffering. (73)

TEN LAST QUESTIONS

Now that you have completed the program, I'd like you to reflect on a series of questions that you probably wouldn't have thought much about before you undertook this anger reduction project.

1. What changes have you identified in your physical well-being since you began this project? Have you seen your blood pressure drop? Do you experience fewer headaches and less stomach discomfort? Are you sleeping better? Do you have more energy?

2. What changes have you been able to make in your use of alcohol or drugs? Are you able to consume fewer or lower doses of prescription medications? Are you better able to relax without the help of medication or alcohol?

3. How have your relationships with family members changed since you started the program? Are you having more fun with your kids? Do people seem more relaxed around you?

4. Are you experiencing more intimacy in your sexual relationship with your partner? Is your partner more interested in being sexual with you? Has sex become more spontaneous and/or more mutual?

5. How has this program affected your relationships at work? Has work become less stressful? Has anyone commented on the "new" you? Do you find it easier to fulfill your responsibilities at work?

6. Have you become more interested and involved in the spiritual aspect of your life? Are you becoming more spiritually aware?

7. How would you describe the reactions of the people around you to the changes you have made in your life? Do you think you are any less manly now that you have a better grip on your temper? Are you any less competitive when it really counts?

8.   What are you still working on? Are there any steps in this program that you are still feeling challenged to accomplish? What situations are most difficult for you as you try to keep your temper on an even keel?

9.   What are you proudest of? What has been your greatest accomplishment? Who shares that sense of accomplishment with you? What was the biggest and most difficult challenge that you have overcome? What have you done to celebrate this?

10. What's next? What do you need to do in order to stay on your new path? Whom can you invite to join you on a similar journey?

PRACTICE, PRACTICE, PRACTICE

You know the old joke about the out-of-towner who asks a New Yorker how to get to Carnegie Hall, right? The answer is practice, practice, practice. I'm sure I don't need to remind you that the same lesson applies to mindfulness. To benefit in a deep and important way from mindfulness you need to make time in your schedule to practice at least several times a week, or even every day of your life.

One last cautionary tale. There was once a rather dim-witted tourist who disappeared in New York City and was found by his worried family several days later clinging to a street post with a sign on the top that said Carnegie Hall. Having searched for Carnegie Hall for hours, the poor fellow thought his quest was over once he had found the sign pointing to his destination.

Mindfulness practice can be a bit like that, too. Mindfulness is not the destination; it is simply a very helpful landmark that points the way to something much greater. It's great and admirable to practice mindfulness and meditation, but the practice by itself is not your destination. Let your practice point the way to your true destination, but don't let the sign become a substitute for the real thing that exists inside the hall. Life awaits!

References

Aquino, K., S. Douglas, and M. J. Martinko. 2004. Overt anger in response to victimization: Attributional style and organizational norms as moderators. *Journal of Occupational Health Psychology* 9:152–64.

Aristotle. 1960. Rhetoric. In *The Rhetoric of Aristotle*, edited and translated by L. Cooper. Englewood Cliffs, NJ: Prentice Hall.

Bankart, C. P. 1997. *Talking Cures: A History of Western and Eastern Psychotherapies*. Pacific Grove, CA: Brooks/Cole Publishing.

———. 2002. Mindfulness as a useful adjunct in therapeutic work with men. *Society for the Psychological Study of Men and Masculinity Bulletin* 7:5–7.

———. 2003. A Western psychologist's inquiry into the nature of Right Effort. *Constructivism in the Human Sciences* 8:63–72.

Benson, H. 1975. *The Relaxation Response*. New York: HarperCollins.

Bhikkhu, A. S. 2000. *Meeting the Monkey Halfway*. York Beach, ME: Samuel Weiser.

Brown, K. W., and R. M. Ryan. 2003. The benefits of being present: Mindfulness and its role in psychological well-being. *Journal of Personality and Social Psychology* 84:822–48.

Cochran, S. V., and F. E. Rabinowitz. 2000. *Men and Depression: Clinical and Empirical Perspectives.* New York: Academic Press.

Csikszentmihalyi, M. 1990. *Flow: The Psychology of Optimal Experience.* New York: Harper Perennial.

Deffenbacher, J. L., E. R. Oetting, and R. A. DiGiuseppe. 2002. Principles of empirically supported interventions applied to anger management. *Counseling Psychologist* 30:262–80.

Del Vecchio, T., and K. D. O'Leary. 2004. Effectiveness of anger treatments for specific anger problems: A meta-analytic review. *Clinical Psychology Review* 24:15–34.

DiGiuseppe, R., and R. C. Tafrate. 2001. A comprehensive treatment model for anger disorders. *Psychotherapy* 38:262–71.

———. 2003. Anger treatment for adults: A meta-analytic review. *Clinical Psychology: Science and Practice* 10:70–84.

Donne, John. 1962. Meditation XVII: Devotions from emergent occasions, 1623. In *Norton Anthology of English Literature.* 5th ed. Edited by M. H. Abrams. New York: W. W. Norton.

Dua, J. K., and M. L. Swinden. 1992. Effectiveness of negative-thought-reduction, meditation, and placebo training treatment in reducing anger. *Scandinavian Journal of Psychology* 33:135–46.

Ellis, A., and R. A. Harper. 1997. *A Guide to Rational Living.* Hollywood, CA: Melvin Powers Wilshire Book Company.

Epstein, M. 1995. *Thoughts Without a Thinker.* New York: Basic Books.

———. 2001. *Going on Being: Buddhism and the Way of Change.* New York: Broadway Books.

Frost, R. 1949. "The Death of the Hired Man." In *Complete Poems of Robert Frost.* New York: Holt, Rinehart, and Winston.

Gaudiosi, J. A. *See* U.S. Department of Health and Human Services.

Gross, J., and R. Levenson. 1993. Emotion suppression: Physiology, self-report, and expressive behavior. *Journal of Personality and Social Psychology* 64:970–86.

Gunaratana, B. H. 2002. *Mindfulness in Plain English*. Boston: Wisdom Publications.

Halgin, R. P., and S. K. Whitbourne. 2005. *Abnormal Psychology: Clinical Perspectives on Psychological Disorders*. 4th ed. New York: McGraw-Hill.

Hammond, W. P., and J. S. Mattis. 2005. Being a man about it: Manhood meaning among African American men. *Psychology of Men and Masculinity* 6:114–26.

Harmon-Jones, E. 2004. On the relationship of frontal brain activity and anger: Examining the role of attitude toward anger. *Cognition and Emotion* 18:337–61.

Hayes, S. C., K. D. Strosahl, and K. G. Wilson. 1999. *Acceptance and Commitment Therapy*. New York: Guilford Press.

Hogan, B. E., and W. Linden. 2004. Anger response styles and blood pressure: At least don't ruminate about it. *Annals of Behavioral Medicine* 27:38–49.

Kabat-Zinn, J. 1994. *Wherever You Go There You Are: Mindfulness Meditation in Everyday Life*. New York: Hyperion.

Kilmartin, C. T. 2000. *The Masculine Self*. 2nd ed. New York: McGrawHill.

Krech, G. 2002. *Naikan: Gratitude, Grace, and the Japanese Art of Self-Reflection*. Berkeley, CA: Stone Bridge Press.

Kwee, M. 1996. Traveling in the footsteps of Hotei towards the 21st century. In *Western and Buddhist Psychology: Clinical Perspectives*, edited by M. G. T. Kwee and T. L. Holdstock. Delft, The Netherlands: Eburon.

Levine, M. 2000. *The Positive Psychology of Buddhism and Yoga*. Mahwah, NJ: Lawrence Earlbaum Associates.

Machiavelli, Niccolo. 2003. *The Prince*. Trans. George Bull. London: Penguin Books.

Martin, P. 1999. *The Zen Path Through Depression*. New York: HarperCollins.

Novaco, R. W. 1996. Anger treatment and its special challenges. *National Center for Post-Traumatic Stress Disorder Clinical Quarterly* 6:3.

Pittman, F. 1993. *Man Enough: Fathers, Sons and the Search for Masculinity*. New York: Berkley Publishing Group.

Pollack, W. 1998. *Real Boys: Rescuing Our Sons from the Myths of Boyhood*. New York: Random House.

Pope, H. G., K. A. Phillips, and R. Olivardia. 2000. *The Adonis Complex: The Secret Crisis of Male Body Obsession*. New York: Free Press.

Potter-Efron, R., and P. Potter-Efron. 1995. *Letting Go of Anger: The 10 Most Common Anger Styles and What to Do About Them*. Oakland, CA: New Harbinger Publications.

Prochaska, J. O. 1999. How do people change, and how can we change to help more people? In *The Heart and Soul of Change: What Works in Therapy*, edited by M. A. Hubble, B. L. Duncan, and S. D. Miller. Washington, D.C.: American Psychological Association.

Reynolds, D. K. 1980. *The Quiet Therapies: Japanese Pathways to Personal Growth*. Honolulu: University of Hawaii Press.

———. 1984. *Constructive Living*. Honolulu: University of Hawaii Press.

Richards, J. C., M. Alvarenga, and A. Hof. 2000. Serum lipids and their relationships with hostility and angry affect and behaviors in men. *Health Psychology* 19:393–98.

Sapolsky, R. M. 1998. *Why Zebras Don't Get Ulcers: An Updated Guide to Stress, Stress-Related Disease, and Coping*. New York: W. H. Freeman and Company.

———. 2004. *Why Zebras Don't Get Ulcers: An Updated Guide to Stress, Stress-Related Disease, and Coping*. 3rd ed. New York: W. H. Freeman and Company.

Smith, M., and B. Houston. 1987. Hostility, anger expression, cardio-vascular responsivity, and social support. *Biological Psychology* 24:39–48.

Snyder, C. R., S. T. Michael, and J. S. Cheavens. 1999. Hope as a psychotherapeutic foundation of common factors, placebos, and expectancies. In *The Heart and Soul of Change: What Works in Therapy*, edited by M. A. Hubble, B. L. Duncan, and S. D. Miller. Washington, DC: American Psychological Association.

Suarez, E., and R. Williams. 1989. Situational determinants of cardio-vascular and emotional reactivity in high and low hostile men. *Psychosomatic Medicine* 51:404–18.

Thomas, S. P. 2003. Men's anger: A phenomenological exploration of its meaning in a middle class sample of American men. *Psychology of Men and Masculinity* 4:163–75.

Thurman, R. A. F. 2005. *Anger*. New York: Oxford University Press.

Thurman, R., and T. Wise. 1999. *Circling the Sacred Mountain: A Spiritual Adventure Through the Himalayas*. New York: Bantam Books.

Troisi, A., and A. D'Argenio. 2004. The relationship between anger and depression in a clinical sample of young men: The role of insecure attachment. *Journal of Affective Disorders* 79:269–72.

U.S. Department of Health and Human Services. Administration on Children, Youth and Families. J. A. Gaudiosi. 2005. Child maltreatment, 2003. www.acf.hhs.gov (accessed April 21, 2005).

C. Peter Bankart, Ph.D., has been actively engaged in his profession as a psychologist since 1971. He received his Ph.D. from Dartmouth College in experimental personality research with a specialty in behavior therapy, and took a job at Wabash College in Crawfordsville, Indiana where he is a senior member of the faculty. He has lived in Japan for several years, taught at Waseda University in Tokyo, and has authored a textbook on the history of psychotherapy, *Talking Cures,* which was published by Brooks/Cole in 1997. In addition to teaching psychology, Bankart directed the student counseling service at Wabash, and has worked as a staff psychologist in a variety of mental health facilities in the United States and Japan.

Some Other
New Harbinger Titles

Depressed and Anxious, Item 3635 $19.95

Angry All the Time, Item 3929 $13.95

Handbook of Clinical Psychopharmacology for Therapists, 4th edition, Item 3996 $55.95

Writing For Emotional Balance, Item 3821 $14.95

Surviving Your Borderline Parent, Item 3287 $14.95

When Anger Hurts, 2nd edition, Item 3449 $16.95

Calming Your Anxious Mind, Item 3384 $12.95

Ending the Depression Cycle, Item 3333 $17.95

Your Surviving Spirit, Item 3570 $18.95

Coping with Anxiety, Item 3201 $10.95

The Agoraphobia Workbook, Item 3236 $19.95

Loving the Self-Absorbed, Item 3546 $14.95

Transforming Anger, Item 352X $10.95

Don't Let Your Emotions Run Your Life, Item 3090 $17.95

Why Can't I Ever Be Good Enough, Item 3147 $13.95

Your Depression Map, Item 3007 $19.95

Successful Problem Solving, Item 3023 $17.95

Working with the Self-Absorbed, Item 2922 $14.95

The Procrastination Workbook, Item 2957 $17.95

Coping with Uncertainty, Item 2965 $11.95

The BDD Workbook, Item 2930 $18.95

You, Your Relationship, and Your ADD, Item 299X $17.95

The Stop Walking on Eggshells Workbook, Item 2760 $18.95

Conquer Your Critical Inner Voice, Item 2876 $15.95

The PTSD Workbook, Item 2825 $17.95

Hypnotize Yourself Out of Pain Now!, Item 2809 $14.95

Call **toll free, 1-800-748-6273,** or log on to our online bookstore at **www.newharbinger.com** to order. Have your Visa or Mastercard number ready. Or send a check for the titles you want to New Harbinger Publications, Inc., 5674 Shattuck Ave., Oakland, CA 94609. Include $4.50 for the first book and 75¢ for each additional book, to cover shipping and handling. (California residents please include appropriate sales tax.) Allow two to five weeks for delivery.

Prices subject to change without notice.